Resilience

One woman's strength, resilience and faith allowed her to find hope and meaning in the midst of adversities

Also by Joan Green

Bridging the Gap, Families in Crisis, Church and Community

Published by Seaview Press; Henley Beach, South Australia. 2001

FolioAvenue Publishing Services

Level 33, Australia Square 264 George Street Sydney, Australia 2000

www.folioavenue.com

ISBN: 978-1-951795-00-9 (sc)

FOLIO AVENUE

Table of Contents

This book is dedicated to my family.

FOREWORD

Joan was the first neighbour I met, as a newlywed. At the time, she was preparing for her own wedding. Our friendship began, when all that happened, over fifty years ago.

During the course of the past half a century, I have witnessed Joan living many of the Fruits of the Spirit. In particular, she has embraced charity, goodness, mildness, modesty and absolute Faith in the Lord, all rolled up in compassion and the wonderful virtue of humanity.

We have supported each other, as we have shared our many joys and sorrows throughout the years.

Joan's memoirs have brought me to a new revelation of the depths of her suffering, unconditional love, strength and appreciation of her life experiences. She seems to be able to realise the blessings that can come from adversity. She is able to wipe the dust from her feet after a storm and get on with her life.

Joan's shared memoirs are part of her true life story. Her story must be read to the end so we can learn the lessons available from her journey through life.

Sometimes her narrative is as raw and painful as salt to a fresh, open wound. Her acceptance and ability to survive and share the joy through sorrow is inspiring.

Positive outcomes are her expectations.

Congratulations to you, Joan, for having the courage to share your experiences and emotions. You are absolutely believable and truly resilient.

From the depths of my heart I thank you for the honour of introducing your life through your book.

Through and with God, all things are possible.

Kathleen (Kathy) McMillan

PREFACE

My life has been like a road map with many roads, lanes and streets, suburbs, towns, cities. I have stayed awhile at one place. Then some change in direction perhaps a holiday or life choice to take a trip. Although I have had the destination in mind and have done all the preparation to get to the destination at the appointed time. The trip may go according to plan. There can also be obstacles.

How I managed these hiccups has depended on my reaction to the crisis. Many things has happened on the journey such as roadwork to hold me up or a detour that has taken me many miles out of the way and to places where I had no idea where I would end up. The journey at times took on a different perspective and unexpected turns.

In my life, I have discovered that no experience has been wasted. Each trial has been a launching pad to a new level spiritually and understanding. My life experiences have shown me how each one has enriched my life.

Every stage of life presented a lesson to be discovered.

"In everything give thanks." 1 Thessalonians 5:18 (NKJV)

I was reminded how the impact that suicide attempts and suicides have on all members of the family after a conversation with a friend whose grandchild had attempted suicide and another grandparent who told me her grandchild had died by suicide. While they are asking what can they do to support their families their grief which can be hidden and often overlooked. Memories came flooding back about my husband's suicide attempts and the unspoken truth, the secrets that went on within the family, friends and work colleagues. There was the pressure not to mention how the person died. The flashbacks were as though it had just happened even though it was twenty three years since the suicide attempt. Surviving the impact of suicide attempts and suicide has given me hope by looking at my own spirituality, hope, meaning and direction. My healing began after my husband died by suicide after he had been missing for six days.

I have found writing has been cathartic in my journey of personal growth and healing. The grief from his suicide attempts and suicide was different to any other grief I had experienced. The sense of isolation and loneliness was insurmountable. Feeling so alone I wrote a poem six weeks after his death. The following year I wrote a thesis on 'Bridging the Gap between families in crisis and the Church and community.' This came out a statement made "I didn't know what to do." This book has come to fruition after a statement "We didn't believe you."

I have realised how the impact of the word suicide had affected any social life as I had known it. Suddenly there were no invitations but hope came after attending a weekend workshop and a weekly program. This began a journey of hope, a search of meaning and direction.

Life went on but the hopes of the future had gone no matter how much I tried to keep going the pain can still be raw at anniversaries. The loss of family, friends, the lack of trust, and the non-belief of what is happening for the person left behind weighed heavily on me. Looking back, it was contact with the chaplain at the scene and the follow up with a psychologist that was the catalyst toward healing and hope for the future. Although I began searching for spirituality, I found common experience within a group environment where I could be vulnerable with talking about loss and grief.

My personal faith has been a major part of my recovery of spirituality, hope, meaning and direction. I had a belief that "with God all things are possible." Matthew 19:26 (NKJV) Today as I walk through life I can trust again with my feelings, emotions, hopes and dreams.

ACKNOWLEDGEMENTS

I wish to acknowledge the help and encouragement I have been given over the years to write my memoirs. In particular I am most thankful to my destiny friends.

Shirley whom I met in my early teens and been a constant person in my life. Kathleen whom I met before I was first married and has spent many hours being a good listener. Patti I have known since my late twenty's. I met Barbara during a time in my life when life was going well and Wendy whom I met when I was going through a difficult time.

Their friendship and willingness to listen without being judgemental has been a great inspiration. The insights that I have gained from talking and listening have been valuable lessons. I have been taught the meaning of life for myself, being true to my soul. The insights that I have gained from talking and listening have been valuable lessons.

Thanks also to the many people who have had confidence in me to tell me to write down what I have come to know while we have been going through crises. I have been so blessed with having my two children who have been there for me and have always encouraged me in my journey of life.

To all who have given me time and encouragement, in particular Gail, Kathleen, and Billie Hunt who have given me much encouragement to keep on with writing my lived experiences. Thank you.

INTRODUCTION

The title of the book "Resilience" is dealing with events that have happened that had changed my life dramatically.

Over the years I have been told many times that I needed to write my story. It is my story, my memories, personal recollections and life experiences to answer the question "How come you are not bitter? It has taken many years to come to a place in my life when I have had time to reflect. Looking back over my life has given me time to reflect and put this in some sort of order. This journey I have travelled has influenced who I am.

A member of a group I was involved with during many years of family trauma once made a statement "We Didn't Believe You" has been a catalyst for me to write my memoirs. If I wasn't believed as an adult; how would a child be heard?

My early memories are of happy times with family and the traditions that were created. There was much joy and laughter being involved with special preparations that were made for Christmas and birthday teas. Early in my childhood I remember having a strong foundation of a love for the Lord. I knew I would find the answers in the Bible. In my paternal grandparents' home, I recall seeing a family Bible, and I saw my grandparents reading it.

A traumatic event at the age of nine happened to me that I kept undisclosed. I didn't have the words and did not tell anyone. A series of events happened before something I couldn't speak about was unleashed. Fifty four years later I reported the crime to the police as I didn't want to take this to the grave.

In the meantime I discovered no matter what happens I could be a voice for change. When it was my story I was able to process it and realised that I could have a voice. This is my season to write down my story and to give back to the community. My ideal would be to share my journey to inspire others to reach their potential. Some lessons I had become able to listen and bloom where I was planted.

This memoir has come out of my journey to get to the stage where I could have a voice that was heard. In my retirement, I have had the opportunity to spend some time back in the area where I had grown up. I believe that no experience in my life had been wasted. I have realised that life experiences and how I have reacted have made me who I am today. Life is exciting. Reflecting on my earlier life I began to see where my strengths had come from and also recognise the weaknesses that I have had to work on during my life.

My strengths kept me going no matter what was happening in my personal world. My main weakness was definitely being afraid to rock the boat and not believing that I had a voice or anyone would listen. As I have listened to people who have been in my care I saw and heard that everyone has a story. If it isn't written down it can be lost forever.

One important lesson that I understood was to reach out and find someone who would listen. It can have an emotional impact on making a change. Through a series of events I become able to take hold of opportunities that came my way. I'd been told many times that I need to write my life story down. In particular how I've come through some death and resurrection experiences without becoming bitter.

I had been able to write and talk about my late husband's death. I was being led to a further healing and knowing that God hasn't given me anymore than I could handle. Hidden trauma had many layers and as memories surfaced it was like peeling an onion one layer at a time before the core of the problem was able to be identified and resolved.

Change was never easy but, from experience, I can say that my life has been full of challenges. These challenges can be a barrier to moving forward when coming to a fork in the road. Dealing with the challenges in life has given me the opportunity to recognise new options and opportunities. I have become able to trust God and to know that He will show me the way when it appears, that there is no way out. It's been listening to that still small voice within and knowing that God has gone before. This has prepared a path ahead. I can take a new road with strength and courage with the knowledge that every challenge in life has been seasonal. There was a new pathway to take in the journey. I need to keep looking forward, not back.

Opportunities can come in unexpected ways. While I was a Community Chaplain and looking for some paid work, employment came from an unexpected source. I received a telephone call from an employment agency asking if I would accept a position looking after an elderly resident at night. Doing sleepovers wasn't on my bucket list but I took the work and that gave me the reference I could get some work in a field of work that I loved. Taking the first step was all it took. I was now living on my own so I so may as well get paid to sleep and be a carer. This also enabled me to continue working as a Chaplain during the day. I had the money to allow me to cover my living costs and to continue what I loved to do. I saw an opening while feeling stuck at the fork in the road. This position gave me a reference for the next employment potential which opened the door to further study.

As I moved forward, being open to my inner healing, I reported a crime to the police that happened fifty four years earlier. I finally acknowledged the trauma that had a grip on my life and when it began to emerge I had the courage to write about what was unfolding. The first time I had been told it was a criminal offence was at a police station. Yes, I was a victim of a crime. What happened to me was finally acknowledged. I finally had the answers and the words to speak about what happened to change the way I interpreted life as a child. It was part of who I am as an adult. I had a name for what happened to me. The question I had was, "Why wasn't I safe?" I should have been safe in my bed. I should not have been made to feel guilty.

How refreshing to be acknowledged and not judged when I was told by the police woman that not only that it was a crime, it wasn't my fault and that I did nothing wrong. It was like the biggest burden had been lifted off my shoulders. I was an innocent nine year old child. I recalled my childhood nightmares of being in a coffin: I was alive, but no one could hear me!

Over the years of going to counsellors, I realised that there is a cost involved in bringing up the subject of sexual abuse. The cost was denial and being told it didn't happen. I would get flashbacks and during those times I would go to talk to a counsellor. On reflection of my life flashbacks began when my daughters turned nine, and finally when my granddaughter turned nine I knew that I had to report it to the police. I would think *"How anyone could hurt a child?"*

The question I had was, "Who believes a child, anyway"? Over the years, I would go home but would leave suddenly. I couldn't understand why I had to leave. When I started to question myself about my behaviour, I recognised that I should talk to a counsellor or go to a support group. I didn't understand why I was behaving like I felt that I need to run. I was feeling anxious and perhaps it was those behavioural patterns like of flight or fight situation. It was fear that kept this secret hidden for so many years.

There were the counsellors who would tell me to "Forgive him" when I even attempted to bring up a memory of the past. The implication was that I was that I was the person to blame and I should not bring up the abuse. I become to realise by their not listening I closed off and felt that I had to slam the lid on it. My emotions shut down. I was feeling vulnerable and closed myself off from expressing myself in case of further rejection. For me there was the part the emotions and body sensations that happen before the memory surfaced.

When I finally knew that I needed to report the crime, I didn't go to a counsellor. I couldn't risk having a Band-Aid put on it -comments like "The incident happened so long ago." My greatest desire was to have closure.

CHAPTER 1
Early Years

My earlier memories were living in an extended family. Our grandparents would visit often. I can remember standing in the cot in the lounge room, beside a window. I was meant to be having a nap. I heard noises, so I stood up to look outside. The voice I heard was my father's. As I looked, I could see a horse beside a tree. My father would drive a horse and sulky to work; as the family didn't get a car until I was around twelve years old. I recall feeling happy when I saw my father home and working in the garden. The garden was some distance from the house.

I remember a new baby coming into the home in the 1940s, where I would watch the baby being bathed. The baby would be dried with a fluffy white towel before being taken outside to get some sun. I would watch as a piece of gauze would be placed on the navel area and a bandage would be bound around the stomach. How times have changed this practice was not done when a baby came into the home in the 1950s.

One time stands out: when a snake had been seen near the bassinet. Aunty took me with her while she checked for any snake eggs. There was a log in the yard near the house that we would play around and sit on. We were looking all around the log to see if we could find any eggs.

Another memory was on Christmas Day, someone got a present that came in a box. We had lots of fun being able to play inside the box. We were all taking turns and there was a lot of laughter.

As the only girl in the family, with three brothers and three male cousins I spent my time with my Aunty when my mother was doing outside chores. The boys had been playing outside and had stopped playing. It was a hot day. Aunty asked me to take oranges to the boys for morning tea. The oranges were placed inside a tea towel, and the corners were gathered together and tied to a strong stick, which I could put over my shoulder. My Aunty made it like I was going on an exciting adventure. I found the boys sitting under the shade of a tree near a fence. They were happy to see me. They were looking for something to quench their thirst. I watched as they all took an orange. The older boys helped the younger ones peel their orange and started to pull the segments apart. I watched as they finished eating the oranges. I returned to the house via the woodheap. I recall my grandfather sitting on the porch and asking me what was I doing as I was to go back inside to my Aunty. Now I realise he would have been concerned about snakes being in the woodheap.

My mother was the second daughter, and she was expected to do all the outside work alongside her father. Her eldest sister had done all the inside work with her mother. Her eldest sister was the only child sent to high school to further studies. As an adult, there was still the expectation for my mother to continue to do what was considered the outside work.

My mother was the one that chopped the wood and milked the cow. The milk was used for the family. Most of the milk would be separated, which in turn gave us cream to make butter. I remember lots of bread and butter custards being made to use any stale bread. I do recall the wonderful taste of the cream that came off the cooled milk after the milk had been boiled on the stove. This was used to go on fruit and sweets as well as on our porridge.

My mother often spoke about being expected to help her father kill cattle for food, as well as being expected to do any other manual labour required outside the home. She was also taught to not have idle hands and could do needlework such as sewing, smocking and embroidery which were some of her many talents.

There was much excitement seeing a person covered up with a hat and a net over her face with a smoking spray in her hand. It was my mother. She had just come back from getting honey from a bee hive that they had found on a tree on the property. We were so happy clapping our hands and laughing together. We just loved eating the honeycomb.

The first time I had seen a man iron clothes was at a neighbour's house, where I was playing with another girl. I must have been about four years old. The baker also came and the bread was what we called a tank loaf. It had a beautiful crust. The tank loaves were two big loaves of bread cooked together. We called the middle when two loaves pulled apart the criss-cross. When the lady was cutting off the crusts, I recall asking for a bit of crust, and she said the crusts are only for the boys; the girls were to have a slice from the criss-cross. This part of the bread where the loaves were pulled apart was soft. I was disappointed it didn't taste the same as the crust.

As I look back over my life and take time to look at where I have come from and where I am today, I can only say that I thank God for allowing the experiences that have happened. My Christian walk began early in my life. As a family we lived in an extended family situation until I was six years old. Spending time with both sets of grandparents and extended family gave me an opportunity to see how different people can get along in the same house.

In the home of my paternal grandparents, there was only one book in the house and it was the Bible. My father's family were brought up Wesleyan. They did not believe in drinking alcohol or doing any work on Sundays.

An incident my mother would talk about was while she was pregnant she had been making clothes for the baby. On a Sunday while doing some smocking she was spoken to about working and was reminded it wasn't done on a Sunday. There was no alcohol, dancing, and no playing cards in the home. I remember hearing adults talking about going to a dry wedding, when there was an abstinence of alcohol at weddings. A person who had made a practice to abstain from drinking alcohol was called teetotaller.

An older cousin has often told me how badly my mother had been treated. Just before I was born, there was an extended family gathering. My father was one of ten children, so there were a lot of people visiting. It was summer and an extremely hot day. Mum's mother-in-law insisted on this young, very pregnant woman be made to go and get enough vegetables to feed the family and visitors. The garden was quite a distance from the house. From the large gathering, no one stepped in to help. My mother was only 19, only a week away from having her third child.

In both homes there was a copper outside for washing. Inside, the stove was a fuel stove heated up by using wood and sticks to start the fire. As children, we would all bring home any sticks we found and some wood for the wood heap, and put it in a place near the house for easy access to use in the fire.

In my early years, I knew that mothers got an allowance from the Australian Government called an endowment for each child. The Child Endowment Act was a Commonwealth legislation which was introduced in 1941, after the birth of her first child. This provided the sum of five shillings a week to the mother until the age of sixteen. There was also a baby bonus, where an amount was given to help the mother's at their time of need. This was a one-off payment. I heard some of the women would use this money to get a pram for the child. It was these payments that helped my mother save to get a Singer sewing machine. I recall my grandmother had a Singer treadle sewing machine but I do not recall my mother being allowed to use it. Before Mum bought her very own treadle sewing machine, she sewed all our clothes by hand. She smocked baby clothes and made underwear and all outer clothes. Socks were knitted. I can even recall the feathers from chickens that had been killed for food being put into a bag to use for filler for eiderdowns and pillows.

I can recall a day in 1950 when my mother bought a treadle sewing machine. Mum had saved her child endowment and brought this machine. Mum was so excited with her new treadle machine. I was fascinated as to how it worked, watching the material passing under the needle and stitches were being made by this machine, Using feet on a pedal to make it go was ever so fascinating. I can recall having my six year old foot on the pedal while watching Mum sit on a chair in the front of the machine. I enjoyed sewing and wanted so much to be like Mum and create things.

This experience was a catalyst to my future as I did enjoy making my clothes from making a pattern, laying it on a piece of cloth and to cut it out. Over the years when my children were small I sewed all their clothes. I spent many hours producing articles of clothing for myself and my children. The excitement to take a piece of material and to the end result was always fascinating to me. Over the years I watched Mum order patterns from a magazine. Mum also made all the boys' clothes, trousers, shirts and nightwear.

My father would go to work in a horse and sulky. He would leave Monday morning and return home after lunch on Saturday. Occasionally he would come home midweek. It was in the late 1950s when my father came home with a car, and began to travel to and from work each day.

Mum was always busy. If not doing chores around the home. Mum kept active in keeping her fingers moving. I remember her having painful fingers and rubbing them together saying that if she didn't keep doing embroidery, smocking, or knitting, the fingers would freeze up.

I was born during the 1940s. I remember people speaking about the Great Depression. It was just after an economic decline when there was a great shortage of food and other essential commodities. I can recall the family talking about coupons that were presented to the shopkeeper when they were buying things such as sugar, tea and butter so each person got his or her share.

To ensure that everyone received a basic amount of essential supplies such as meat, butter, sugar and tea, the government brought in a system of rationing. Everyone had to apply for ration books, which contained a number of coupons. Each coupon gave the holder permission to buy a certain amount of something, usually over a weekly period. Despite the hardship, rationing was well received by the public because it applied to everyone equally. There was also a clothing ration.

It was a time when people worked together to share what they had to make things easier. I recall clothes being unpicked and ironed and the material used to make a new outfit. Flour bags were used for pillowslips as well as being used as material to sew clothing. Sugar bags were used for foot towels. "Repair, reuse, make-do, and don't throw anything away" was a motto I grew up with. Clothes were handed down. Socks were knitted and clothes were mended and at times with cloth placed over holes in clothing and sewn on. Clothes were recycled and reused. People became very resourceful in all they did to have a good life. I remember our parents made everything fun and we enjoyed our life and what we had. If a new item came into the house there was much rejoicing. I didn't hear anyone complaining about their lot in life. People found happiness and contentment while being resilient in the midst of uncertainty.

There was a great respect for people. Out of respect men dipped their hats to greet or acknowledge a person. This was done out of respect between two people. When a funeral passed everyone would stop and wait until the procession had passed. The men would take their hat off and bow their head in a sign of respect. Men were addressed as Mister, boys were addressed as Master, girls were addressed as Miss and married folk as Mr and Mrs, and this was a mark of respect. Each person was treated equally. Unmarried women were called Miss. Good manners at the table and saying Grace before meals were a must for our family. I remember struggling to learn to use a knife and fork and a neighbour, who was visiting, saw that I was struggling and took the time to show me how to hold the utensils for eating.

When we arrived home from school we knew our mother would be there. If she wasn't, we would have known something serious must have happened. My mother did the washing, ironing, cleaning, cooking, mending garments, and clothes making for the family, as well as managing the family budget. There was no bakery in the area, so bread was made at home. Fresh bread was made with yeast that was made from potatoes. I remember the big bags of flour. We watched as the dough would rise. Walking past bread shops remind me of the smell of home baked bread.

While growing up in the country, I saw that when there were a problem people, would rally around and help out. When a farmer had a crisis people turned up to milk the cows because that had to be done. Others would drop off food, mind the children, sit and listen, post letters and ensure that the family had some cash to get by. I witnessed what was done and the potential of what can be done within a community.

By the time I was six years old, my family had moved into our own home. Mum told us many times how she had saved the endowment payments and was able to buy the house on five acres for our family to live in. In the 1950s, my mother had been able to budget and save money, however, the solicitor told her that it was to go in my father's name. The solicitor told her she could only own a sewing machine.

This was the year I started school and began to attend Sunday school. Although both parents were brought up as Protestants, they attended different denominations. My father's family would attend church, and the only book I saw in their house was a Bible, and Sunday was a total day of rest. My mother was brought attending church, and Sunday was for families to get together to enjoy a baked lunch and a do what one wanted to do in the afternoon as long as it was quiet.

In the country, we walked to the church. The highlight of my week was going to Sunday school and learning about God. We committed to memory the Catechism and Bible verses. Each week we would learn a line or two of the Catechism. I understood that "I was made a Member of Christ, A child of God and an Inheritor of the Kingdom of Heaven" (Anglican Catechism 1662). I recall going home from the church singing "Walking and leaping and praising God" Acts 3:8 (NKJV). "Jesus loves me, this I know; for the Bible tells me so, little ones to Him belong. They are weak but He is strong" (attributed to Anna Bartlett Warner). When I didn't feel loved or that anyone cared about me, I would sings these words and have a sense of peace. I committed to memory the Lord's Prayer and it was the basis for my prayers.

The Lord's Prayer

Our Father which art in heaven, Hallowed be thy name,
Thy kingdom come, Thy will be done in earth, as it is in heaven
Give us this day our daily bread
And forgive us this day our debts, as we forgive our debtors.
And lead us not into temptation, but deliver us from evil:
For thine is the kingdom
And the power, and the glory, forever Amen
- (Matthew 6:9-13 ((NKJV)

During the week, my brothers and I attended school. To reach the school, we walked on a well-worn track through the bush. Sometimes while walking to school we would meet up with other children along the way. As we walked together, we would go over and chat about the lessons we had in school during the day. It was always a happy time. We would count to one hundred and go through the alphabet. If anyone was struggling with the work, we would encourage them in their learning. I don't think we knew that was what we were doing; we all helped each other to do the best we could.

When the trees were flowering, we would pick flowers to take to the teacher, and we would be able to leave school a few minutes earlier than the rest of the class. I can remember Wattle Day being celebrated. At the beginning of spring, the wattle would be blossoming, and we loved to see it in the buckets that the teacher would put the blooms at the front of the classroom. Wattle is a tree that grows throughout the country. The golden wattle is known as a symbol of unity and resilience, and it is said to represent the people who live in Australia. We would look for birds, and my favourite one was listening to the laughter of the kookaburra; I loved watching it as it stood with dignity on a high branch of a tree.

Empire Day was a great day of celebrations. It celebrated Queen Victoria's birthday on 24th May each year. We would get tyres from the local timber mill and roll them home to put on the bonfire. We would gather sticks and branches from trees that had fallen. We celebrated by having half a day at school. I can still see the older children who went to High school coming back to school for a half day. The last celebration of Empire Day took place in 1958. I missed the celebrations as Empire Day was an opportunity for students to unite with the children who had gone on to high school. I found it was encouraging to see the big kids come back to our school. They were the vision of the stepping stone we could take to go on to further education; not everyone went on to high school. The bonfires were a community affair. Not all children went on to high school; some stayed and completed the final years at the primary school. The bonfires were also a community affair.

When I was eight, we moved to live in a cottage beside the railway line. My mother took on work as a railway gatekeeper opening and closing manual traffic gates each time a train was passing. The gates would be closed when a train was due and opened between times. Each morning the telephone would ring and she would be given the timetable for the day. She did this to supplement the income as she wanted to save enough to get a bathroom built. The house was being rented to another railway family.

With moving to the cottagc near the railway line meant we lived on a main road into town, this meant we had services that we had not had before. Bread was delivered from a local bakery. Bread did not have preservatives in it; when it became stale, we would use it up by making bread and butter pudding, which would be served with homemade custard. I loved bread and milk sprinkled with sugar. Food was never wasted. The butcher came around weekly, and a fisherman came on a Friday. One night a week, a van selling honey and small goods would call. We were one of the last deliveries at the end of the day. The greengrocer would sell fruit and vegetables. Sometimes we able to get an ice cream in a cone as a treat.

Ice would be delivered once a week and would be held by tongs to deliver it to the ice chest. Mostly we would get a block of ice that was too big, and we would take turns sitting on the floor using a saw to cut the block to size. Over the course of the day the ice would slowly melt. There was a drip tray under the chest that was to be emptied regularly.

The postie would deliver mail. I recall when the postie would deliver mail twice a day. Receiving a letter was the highlight of the day. On Sundays a paper was delivered, and he would spend the afternoon reading the paper; I would be given the comic pages and was able to do the puzzles. I have such happy memories of doing all the puzzles and competitions. It was such a thrill when I received certificates in the mail with gold stars on them.

About once a month a man would come around selling products. He would have a bag stocked with salve, ointments and other products such as a tapioca pudding, which was a family favourite.

A new school was built in the local village closer to where we lived. We walked along the side of the road to go to school. I do remember having to take water to school as we didn't have any water in the tank at the new school. We had the freedom to be children. There was a sense of community and people looked out for each other. "It takes a village to raise a child" was achieved. If we did anything wrong, everyone knew everyone else, and our parents would have heard about it. There was no chance that we could get away with anything.

A ball with a piece of timber (if there was no bat) that would create a game of cricket or rounders. We would use what we would find to use to create something. Using branches from trees would be used to make a tepee around a tree. One of the games we played was hopscotch, which was a lot of fun. We only had a hard surface, a piece of stick or thin wood to draw the squares and at the end a box to turn around in. We had a scotch which would be a small stone picked up from the road to throw into a square. The idea was to help with our balance and hop on one leg to the box at the end, turn around and come back. I would watch my brothers playing jacks. They used knucklebones, which is a bone in the ankle of a sheep, which was thrown up and caught in various manners. They also played marbles and would swap marbles with their friends. At school one of the games we played were called farmer in the dell. We would sit around in a circle singing farmer in the dell, where the farmer takes a wife and in turn pick farmers, children, or animals. We skipped, and if we had two ropes or an extra-long one, we would divide it in two and begin twirling the rope in opposite directions.

Cooking cakes and baking biscuits would leave a beautiful aroma in the home. The aroma was very inviting when mum baked while we were at school. We often came home to that sense of warmth and welcoming. Christmas tradition was important. We knew when it was six weeks before Christmas when the fruit cakes and plum puddings would be made. The plum pudding would be wrapped in a specially prepared cloth. When the pudding was cooked there would be a coating between the pudding and the cloth. The pudding would be hung until it was ready to be used. Before it was eaten, the pudding would be boiled again. The Christmas cake would be sprinkled with either orange or some spirits, depending on who would be eating the cake.

Just before Christmas, the school holidays would begin for a six week break. It was the time of the year when fruit was plentiful. We had our own plum trees, lemon tree, persimmons, and grapes. My father would bring home fruit when it was plentiful from near where he was working. We would get a hand of bananas, bags of oranges and limes, mangos as well as Nashi (also known as China) pears. All hands on deck when it was time to preserve the fruit. As usual, Mum had a way of getting us all involved with peeling fruit, washing the jars, and getting enough wood to keep the wood burning stove. There was always a competition to see if we could put down more bottles of preserves than the previous year.

Leading up to Christmas, it became quite a game of going to find a branch to use to clean the chimney for Santa to come down. Oh, how Mum could make everything we did fun. Paper chains would be made for decorations for the tree and the house. The paper chains would be made out of crepe paper. The edge of folded newspaper would be cut in shapes and would be place on shelves. Glue was made from flour and water. We made many streamers that went across the room, hanging them from corners. There was a pine tree in the front yard, which we would decorate. When that tree grew too big, we would go out to select a suitable tree to decorate. This tree would have been placed in a bucket tin a corner of the room. We would use pine cones, and place in a tray as a centre piece on the sideboard, and pick Christmas bush for table decorations. It was a tradition for an aunty to bring Christmas bells from her farm. It was a bell-like flower, which varied from pure yellow to deep red and yellow tips. After Christmas some of the decorations would be taken down and folded up and put away for the following year.

Christmas day was a day of fun. We'd wake up extremely early and get our present. We would be playing with the gift before the sun was up. I do recall getting a stroller one year, and went walking up and down the road outside our house thinking I was a mother and taking my doll for a walk. The children would all go to Sunday school while our parents prepared lunch. Two great-uncles would come each Christmas day. They had a small suitcase which they carried when they came to visit. After they got settled with a drink and some cake, they would sit on a chair and happily hand out gifts. They would lift the lid and we would all get excited to see what was in the small suitcase before proceeding to pass out a handkerchief for each person who was there. I received a single handkerchief until I was twelve, then I started to receive a nice box of handkerchiefs. We got so excited over the small things. I remember the excitement of receiving a cake of nice-smelling soap. Balloons were another favourite gift that we received. Lunch was a baked chicken and vegetables from the garden. Dessert was all homemade, plum pudding, custard and cream. After we got electricity, we would make ice-cream. I remember the beautiful aromas that came from the plum pudding, which had been made in a cloth, are brandy put over the pudding and lit with a match, and we enjoyed watching the flames. The excitement of eating the dessert was finding threepenny bits in the plum pudding. That tradition finished once the decimal currency came in as the coins were no longer suitable to place in the plum pudding.

For the Christmas season, we made a refreshing drink which was great to drink on a warm day. It was ginger beer. It tasted of ginger, and I remember the plant was fermented with a mixture of yeast, ginger syrup, lemon juice and water. This was put into the bottles to store. The bottles were lined up against the wall. Occasionally the bottles would explode. The bottle top would come off and fizzy drink would go all over the room.

The animals we had included chooks, an Australian slang word for chickens. There were several hens and one rooster. I can recall the rooster crowing early in the morning. This became the alarm clock for us to wake up to. We would have a regular supply of eggs for eating, and some were left in the nest when a hen decided to sit on and hatch a clutch of eggs. This he was called a broody hen and would sit on the eggs day and night, leaving once daily to eat, drink and poop. If anyone tried to remove her from her eggs she would hiss at you and peck you. When the hen stopped producing eggs, it was a sad time for them as we would find one cut up on our dinner table when there was a special occasion. Special occasions included Easter, Christmas, and birthday dinners. Collecting the eggs from the henhouse was excitement to find eggs, in particular if the hens laid eggs while scratching around outside the hen coup. The hens were free range except when they went to roost at night, and the gate was closed mainly to keep out foxes.

Monday was always wash day, and the water was not wasted; it was then used for washing the floors. The copper continued to be used to wash clothes. The clothes would be sorted with the whites being washed first, the coloured, dark and lastly towels. The copper was outside, and we would use a copper stick to pull out the clothes, trying not to waste water and being careful not to be burned by the boiling water. The articles would be rinsed in cold water and wrung out before being placed on the clothes line. If the white clothes would get a bit yellow, a Reckitts blue bag was added to the rinsing water. The blue bags made the clothes white again. Over the years, the irons used in the family changed. We started with a flat iron which had been heated on the stove; I would watch as Mum would iron a piece of material to get any black off from the stove before ironing starched cloth. After electricity came, we used an electric iron and, later, a steam iron.

Water was a resource that was to be used sparingly, so the hot water from washing the clothes would be used to wash the wooden floors. I can still see my mother on her knees, scrubbing floors with a brush and sandsoap. Monday night's dinner was meat left over from Sunday roast. Bubble and squeak, made from the leftover vegetables, was a favourite meal.

I remember the excitement when a washing machine was delivered. This machine was loaded from the top and over the top was a wringer to wring the water out of the clothes. Finally, Mum didn't need to use her hands to wring the water out of the clothes.

Tuesdays were for ironing. The clothes were all starched. Before the clothes were ironed, the items were laid out, and sprinkled with water and rolled up. We thought it was funny when we saw the clothes being washed; drying on the line, the dry washing brought in;

and the starched clothes sprinkled with water, rolled up, and left for ironing.

Another day was put aside for baking biscuits and cakes for lunches. Anytime there were extra vegetables or fruits, there would be fresh jam, pickles and, chutney.

Christmas and special birthdays were the only time we got a case of soft drinks to share with family and any visitors. We thought we were special, being able to have something we hadn't made. It was a reward for all of us helping while we made memories of growing up in our family. Liquorice allsorts and nuts in the shell were also a tradition that we had on the table at Christmas.

I found school exciting. I did enjoy walking to school in bare feet. When a new school was built closer to where we lived, we walked to school on a dirt road where we attended Sunday school. I recall the only time we wore shoes was to Sunday school or a special outing. Most of the children went to school barefoot. Because I was a girl, I was to wear a hat to Sunday school. I recall my mother saying she was spoken to after my first day at Sunday school because I wasn't wearing a hat.

We were taught to sew at school by doing samples of all the stitches and types of hems. By the time I was thirteen, I became skilled at making a pattern and sew my own clothes. I loved sewing and found it fun.

When a couple were about to get married, a kitchen tea was held for everyone in the community. A community notice would be broadcast over the local radio station, and we would all go to the local hall. Dancing was wonderful. The musicians were a man playing the drum, and a lady playing the piano accordion. The adults would play euchre in the kitchen area while the dance was on. Midway through the evening, supper would be provided by the ladies. I can recall the social events included a country and western singers coming to the community hall. At times movies nights were held and we could buy a small chocolate during the interval.

By the time I turned eight my two paternal grandparents had died. My grandmother died in Hospital when I was eight, in 1952, my grandfather had died four years before. One of the things I thank my parents for was we were taken to the funeral of our paternal grandmother. When our grandfather died, it was kept from the children. I can't recall anyone speaking about his death, although we knew he was in hospital. My grandfather died during the time my mother was pregnant with her fifth child.

When my paternal grandmother died the children were all able to go to the funeral. At the cemetery, we stood together watching the ceremony from under the shade of a large tree. We loved it. Knowing that there was a place we could visit to be near Nan. I noticed how the adults were dealing with the loss differently. All were dressed in black; most of the people were stoic. One person became quite upset, and I remember we talked about it. I can only recall good memories about the day, and all the family were together celebrating Nan's life.

CHAPTER 2

Loss of Innocence Secret

Growing up with a loving family I had felt safe. My mother was always aware of keeping me safe as a young girl. Being an only girl with brothers she constantly told me, "Girls inside, boys outside."

No matter how much a parent tries to protect her children, she is not with them all the time. Children go to bed to sleep in their own bed. In those days, there were no locks on windows, or doors. It was during my ninth year that I lost my innocence. It wasn't by anyone in the family or a regular visitor. It was someone outside our circle of friends. I knew who the person was as I had heard his name and had seen the person within the community.

While sleeping in my own bed, in my own room I expected to be safe. My parents would have assumed that I would be safe during the night. However, I woke in my bed with a man on top of me doing things I could not put into words. He held me down and told me to relax. I was terrified. He warned me not to tell anyone, claiming if I told, I would be sent away. Fear took over and I shut down. I didn't want to be sent away. Having no words and not feeling safe, I blocked the incident out of my mind. I had a life changing-experience that changed the course of my life. I had kept the experience a secret for so many years. Who would believe me? As a nine year old, I didn't know the words to use to tell anyone.

However, my life had changed from being an innocent child to a person who became hypervigilant. I wouldn't go to bed without the room being checked. I would take a torch and read to keep myself awake so I would be able to protect myself. Somehow I thought that if I kept a blanket over my head no one would know that I was there. I had pains in my stomach. I had pains in my stomach and my parents were concerned about them. I was taken to the Doctor, who sent me to hospital. The reason for my abdominal pain was put down to constipation. The treatment included giving a nine year old child an enema. I remember screaming and telling them no. I was held down, and the procedure was forced on me. Looking back, that experience was just as traumatic as the sexual abuse. In those days, parents were sent home and weren't encouraged to stay with their children while they were in hospital. I know after that experience in the hospital, I found it hard to trust women.

During this period in my life, I held onto my faith. I knew that Jesus loved me. I hung onto my childlike faith. When I was ten years of age, I had been unwell. My father was going into town on the bus. He asked me what I would like him to bring home for me. I asked my father to bring me a Bible. This was my first Bible, and I carried with me wherever I travelled

Before the bathroom was installed in our previous home, my mother fell pregnant with her sixth child. This changed the dynamics in the home. I recall how sick Mum had been during the pregnancy. We all took on new responsibilities in the home. Six weeks before the birth of the baby the doctor wanted Mum to be close to the hospital. My sister was born when I was ten years old. My brothers would tease me constantly about being the only girl. When my father came to tell me I had a sister all I could say "I'm not the only girl". That felt good. Somehow I thought having her share my room no one would come in. However I was constantly vigilant at night hearing every rustle of the trees outside the bedroom window.

During this time wherever I saw my mother, her hands were constantly busy making baby clothes. She would begin smocking to make clothes for the baby and do embroidery on little matinee jackets, nighties and dresses. As children, we were not told when there was to be a new baby in the house. I remember going home during lunch at school to collect something I had forgotten and saw my mother cutting out material. She was making baby nighties. She quickly covered up what she was working on hoping I hadn't seen it. Children were definitely brought up being seen and not heard. We were never allowed to listen to adults when they had visitors.

During the time my mother was away from home, two young ladies came into the house to look after the children and to do the work my mother had been doing. They were just as excited as the rest of the family that my mother would be bringing home a baby. One of the girls would be knitting baby outfits and making rosebuds to go on the jackets. There was much anticipation waiting for the new baby as I was shown how to make rosebuds to go on a jacket. I was made part of the preparation for Mum to come home with my sister.

Remembering the house on five acres was in my father's name. My father was able to do what he liked with it without consulting my mother. While my mother was in town waiting to have the baby, my father sold the family home. This was a life-shattering experience for my mother. She had worked so hard to make a home for the family only to have my father sell it. This experience just implanted in my mind that a woman had no rights when it came to finance in a marriage.

When I was ten years old, my friend Jessica suddenly went to live with her grandmother in the city. I didn't know why she went away for many years, but I later heard that her baby sister had died. My friend was one of fourteen children. She told me after we met in later life that she had been very upset about the loss of her sister. Her grandmother had been visiting during this time and thought she was doing the right thing when she was returning to the city and took Jessica to live with her. It was not explained to me, and I thought I must have done something wrong for her to go away.

I met Virginia as she would walk to my house every morning before school. Virginia would stop at my home and we would walk together; when we went to high school, we travelled by bus. We became best friends. Virginia had a health problem and went to the hospital to have surgery. During the surgery, Virginia died. It was the last day of my first year at High school. I was twelve years old.

On the day before the surgery, I visited Virginia in the hospital to. Virginia was sitting up on the bed and was happy to chat and talk about the operation that she was having the next day. It was also the last time I saw Virginia. It was the last sport afternoon before school ended for the year. Sport finished early, and I had to walk past the hospital on the way back to school. It was a serious offence if I had been caught out as there were strict rules at the school. However, I decided to sneak in to see her in the ward. I am glad we did get to talk that last time.

I remember feeling a loss as I walked out the door to leave the hospital.

It was the school holidays, and we didn't live close by it would have been difficult not see her again for at least six weeks, before school started back. Virginia and her family would usually spend time in the city during school holiday breaks. I was sitting alone on a seat on the bus, waiting to go home from school, when a girl from her class approached me to let me know that the Headmaster had come to the class to tell the students that Virginia had died during the surgery. She just told me the news and walked away. I was in shock. My friend had died, and I wouldn't see her anymore. It was hard to take it in.

When I arrived home, I told my mother. She was so upset and began to cry. When I saw how upset my mother was, my own emotions shut down. I watched my mother crying. I felt as though my feelings weren't important. I waited for a time, turned around and went to my room to cry alone. My mother made no effort to talk to me about it. I felt that I was being ignored in my grief. Virginia had been my best friend and she had died. I was at a loss. I was twelve years old and I felt that I couldn't talk to anyone about the loss of a friend. There was no one to console me. I felt alone in my grief. It was like Virginia hadn't lived. It was a sad time for me.

I was not able to talk to anyone about life-changing events I discovered, but I discovered that it would come up at a later time. Many years later, it took one traumatic event to bring the two events to the surface, and I felt safe enough to talk to someone. I came to know that one traumatic event can start to open a can of worms in relation to events that haven't been spoken about. One of these memories was the death of my friend, Virginia and I was finally able talk about my friend and to grieve the loss.

CHAPTER 3

The Teenage Years

During my teenage years, a family moved into the district. They had a daughter my age and we became good friends. The family stayed three years. This family had such a positive influence on my life. The father looked after the farm. While the mother would travel each day on the bus to do voluntary work in a residential place for people with disabilities. She loved doing the washing and ironing for the organisation. The family became part of the church community. As there was no fellowship group for teenage girls a group commenced. The fellowship was called Girls Friendly Society. It had the motto "Bear one another's burdens and so fulfil the law of Christ". (Galatians 6:2 (NKJV)

The group members were peers at the school I attended. We could meet once a week in the local hall. We had outings with another group that was nearby. Without this group, we would have only seen each other at school as we all lived a distance away from each other. Some of the activities that included were bushwalking.

We went walking up the side of a mountain close to the area we lived. On another adventure, we walked through a field, went to the river, and met a boat that collected milk from the farmers to take to a milk factory. At the end of this beautiful ride on the milk boat, we went through the factory to see what happened to the milk after it arrived at the factory. This family certainly left an indelible imprint on my spiritual journey

The person who sexually abused me as a nine year old returned in my fourteenth year. He approached me when I was a teenager walking home after an evening of meeting for the fellowship group. I had spent the evening in a safe environment. As the evening came to an end, we all said good night. The girls who lived close by and lived in the village parted ways. Three of us walked in the opposite direction. Along the road we were walking we came to a lane where my two friends parted. I continued along the road to home. We were still happy after an evening of fun and fellowship.so we joyously said good night and went our separate ways. I had no reason to be concerned or scared as I had walked home alone before many times. Occasionally I would hear the hoot of an owl and rustling of the bushes from the wind. Light would come from the moonlight. On previous occasions, I had not seen a car while walking home at that time of night. It was a quiet night. On opposite sides of the road, there was bush and trees that would be protection for anyone who wanted to hide in the growth.

I heard a noise a short distance after I left my two friends. A person came out of the bushes and grabbed me. I screamed and froze. I was terrified and just stood there on the spot, too frightened to move. I knew who it was. He had returned. Fear stopped me. I was so naïve I still didn't know the words to say. Things happen in my life that has been a way out of a bad situation, and this was one of those times. In the distance, I saw a light coming closer and over the hill car lights were beginning to show. The person told me to stay there and he raced into the bushes. I was frozen on the spot, not knowing what to do. As the car was passed, I remember the thoughts that were going through my head. What if the person in the car decided to do something to me if I stopped the car? As I was gathering my thoughts the car passed me. I made a decision to run as fast as I could home praying he would not come after me. When I arrived home everyone was in bed. I went straight to my bedroom and slept under the bed that night.

The following day when I got to school, I tried to talk to my two friends who had left me at the lane the evening before. They began laughing and telling others about me screaming, and how they just ran home. They were making such a joke about the incident I didn't tell them what had happened to cause me to scream. Again I kept it a secret.

This incident was the first time he had approached me since I woke finding him on top of me as a nine year old. Again, I didn't tell anyone what had happened. Looking back, there must have been some change in my behaviour. My mother started to come to the community hall to meet me and walk home with me after that incident. I do believe that I was being looked after by a power greater than anything I could have planned I was protected. I had a choice to make: stay or run. I ran.

Later that year I was given a wonderful opportunity to go to a Bishop's Enthronement in a regional city. The leader of the fellowship group was able to get three tickets to the event so I felt that it was a special thing to be chosen. We travelled in the train during the night arriving at our destination at around 3a.m.

We woke early and had breakfast. During the day, we visited a radio station, and went for a walk along the promenade at the beach. Later in the day, we walked up a steep hill to visit the Cathedral where the Bishop's Enthronement was to be held. We stayed for a church service and met up with Ministers who we had met before. Upon arriving back at our accommodation, the adults spent the evening talking. My friend and I were told we could try on clothes that were in the wardrobe of their daughter, Jane, who was out for the evening. When Jane arrived home, we were modelling the outfits for the family. Jane joined in, and we had a singalong. The evening was such fun having much talking, singing, and laughter.

The following day, we spent time visiting a lake. I remember getting cuts in my feet from the sharp stones when we went swimming. After returning home for an evening meal, we ended the night with another singalong. Sunday morning we had a quick breakfast before we left for the Cathedral. We attended the church service. After the service, we went for a tour of the Cathedral while we listened to the broadcast of the Bishops Enthronement.

In the evening, we attended the Cathedral for a service. We dressed in our uniforms and joined up with other girls who were in the fellowship from other church parishes. There were 2,500 people who attended and welcomed the Bishop. Before the address by the Bishop, clergy spoke of their loyalty, laity and youth of the diocese. Bishop Housden said "Mine is a lonely life". The Bishop was surrounded by friends and felt our loyalty. After the service, we met the Bishop and his wife.

We felt so privileged to be able to attend this event. It left an impact on my life. The following morning we packed our belongings into a suitcase and left for the railway station to go home.

As I was the first person in the family to attain the intermediate certificate, my father promised to buy me a watch. I was so looking forward to receiving it from him. To my amazement, my Uncle came in a taxi to give me a watch he had brought for me. I started to cry. I felt as though my father was cheated out of buying the watch. I wanted to get it from my father. However, on my fifteenth birthday, my father came home with a necklace and earring set for me to wear to dances. I was also given some money to buy a special pair of shoes for going out. It was a special day.

During my fifteenth year two other girls and I took part in the passion play presenting the passion of Jesus Christ, his trial and his death. It was a part of Lent. It was put on with the combined churches. I recall going each Saturday for many weeks to rehearse our parts in the play. The parts we were playing were the three angels. What an exciting thing to do. It left a legacy of memories.

I was confirmed in the Anglican Church, this strengthened my personal relationship with God. I remember kneeling in front of the Bishop, and as he anointed my forehead with the sign of the cross and placed his hand on my head I became a full member of the church. I felt a wonderful sense of peace. It was a very special day in my life. The following Sunday during the Eucharist, we received our first holy communion. I felt a sense of purpose in my Christian walk with God. Knowing that Jesus loved me no matter what happened in my life. Someone loved me!

The sports that I played at school were tennis, basketball, and hockey. I played for one year on a team in the district for hockey. I received a cup and a cup and saucer for the being part of the team. I enjoyed watching games of football and hockey at the local parks.

During my formative years a neighbor, Doreen, became a special person in my life. She was a real mentor. It was a really special treat to visit her. I would sit on a chair while she prepared biscuits and cakes. There was no running water or sink; water was not plentiful as we all had tanks. To wash dishes, we used a large bowl. After she finished preparing the biscuits, she placed the trays in the oven of a fuel stove. The utensils were washed, in readiness to begin again. To this day, I wash up as I go, and that habit is from watching and learning the skill from her.

Not only did we share the love of cooking, but we would also inspect the garden. If there was a weed to be found, I would be allowed to pull a few. I would see her walking along the road with bunches of flowers to go to her church to make arrangements and place in the church for the Sunday service. As I watched this lady live her life she showed me about being faithful to what she believed in by her actions. It is with sadness I do not recall having told her how much she meant to me. My valued friend was there as I was growing up. She was always kind to a child, and as the years went by, we were able to share from the heart what the Lord was doing in our respective lives.

It was while I was attending a church service when I heard of her passing. It was a shock to hear the news, but all those wonderful moments we shared came rushing back. I do know that this beautiful lady will be with her Lord. We kept in touch over the years. I valued the input that she put into my life and she will never know how much she meant to me. She inspired me in so many ways and lived her life well.

CHAPTER 4
Leaving Home

I felt as though home wasn't a safe place for me. We didn't have any locks on the doors. There were no locks on the windows. I would be so anxious about going to bed. I would continue to ask my father to check under the bed and in the wardrobe.

I enjoyed cooking the dinner for the family. There were nine people to cook for. My father comes to know not to ever tell me he enjoyed the meal when my mother was about. When dad told me how much he enjoyed the meal, it became an open door for Mum to look for faults about what I didn't do right. My mother and I were clashing all the time. Upon looking back, I know she only wanted the best for me. We had difference of opinion in how things were done. No matter what I did, she had another way of doing it. There was always something that I did wrong-I didn't iron right; I didn't wash right, or I didn't act right. In the end, we didn't do things the same way.

While still at school in the early 1960s, I heard that there was work for student nurses at the local hospital. It was a holiday weekend, and we were visiting my maternal grandparents at the beachside when I made a decision to go to a telephone booth and made a call to speak to the Matron at the hospital. I asked if there was a position available. She told me to come in for an interview the following Tuesday. Without saying anything to my parents I went to school, and told the headmaster that I would be leaving the school for an interview. He signed me off so I could leave the school to go to the appointment.

Matron began the interview by laying out the rules as to what would be was expected of me. The rules included what could be worn, and how a young person was to conduct herself. Matron came across as a person who would be not only firm but fair. One of the rules included was that slacks were not to be worn at any time. After the interview Matron showed me around, took me to see the room where I would have accommodation. I went to the sewing room, and was measured for a uniform, and aprons required for my new role as a student nurse. I could start on the Thursday, only two days away.

I went home and told my mother I had found work, and could live in the nurse's quarters. Meals would be provided as well as a kitchen, where I would be able to make a snack. There was a laundry where I could do my own washing. When we were having dinner, I told my father. It was a relief when there was no opposition to me leaving home. The following day my bag was packed. Mum and I found a suitable piece of material to make two pair of new pyjamas to take with me. Fortunately, I already had black stockings and black shoes as they were part of my school uniform. I felt a sense of pride in the uniform which was a striped dress, starched apron, collar, and belt. I would wear the red cape to and from work.

On accepting the position I went to live-in the nurses' quarters that was linked to the hospital by a covered walkway. Matron mentioned that she had the flat just inside the front door. I wanted to talk at any time I could knock on her door. So my journey into nursing began, and I loved the work. As a student, I was taught how to work in the pan room to sterilise the pans. They were made shiny after they were sterilized. While the pan was hot a white powder was put on the pan, and a cloth was used to shine the pans with a cloth. We had a roster. Early morning starts began at 6am. However if we wanted to complete the showers we all started at 5.30a.m, and often didn't complete the work until breakfast was nearly over, so we would run, and have a quick breakfast. Under no circumstances could we be late on the ward for the next part of our shift.

New students worked in the sterilisation room. Cleaning the pans was a start. Every three months we did a stint of night duty. The youngest student was to cook the meal for the night staff which they were to eat around 2:00 a.m. It was something that I enjoyed doing, and would get some good comments about my cooking.

Matron took no nonsense - one wrong move and a young student was no longer part of the team. No one talked about the reasons the student had left. Friendships began only to be lost. There were no explanations given. Life went on. There was no looking back.

I certainly didn't want to go breaking the rules. When I was called to Matron's office, I had no idea what it could be about. I understood that the only thing I had done that was against the rules was try on a pair of slacks. We often tried on each other's clothes, and we were more than willing to do so. Another student had been home on her days off, and had been making some new clothes. One of the items of clothing was a pair of slacks that her sister had made. Of course I knew that wearing a pair of slacks was against the rules. The desire to see what it would be like to wear them was too strong. When the front doorbell rang, I went downstairs, and poked my head out so that no one would me. But Matron had seen me, I had forgotten about her flat was just near the front door. What started off as trying on a pair of slacks as a bit of fun became having done something that broke the rule of not wearing slacks. The consequence of this action was not being able to go out socially for twenty eight days; I could only go to work, and go back to the nurses' quarters. I was not to even go out to the shop across the road from the hospital. There were no excuses.

I come to know first-hand how Matron was a person of her word. The rules were there not to be broken. There was a consequence if a rule was broken. Fortunately, at this time I was not sacked. Today you may laugh at this rule, but in the 1960s it was a serious breach of the rules to wear slacks by students within the community or inside this particular hospital setting.

During the next three years, three family members died. My maternal grandfather was a patient in the hospital where I worked. It was difficult watching him deteriorate in health. The night he died, I was at home with my parents when the call came through. When I was eighteen, I was home for the evening when a telephone call came to tell my mother her youngest sister had had a baby. My parents' left for the hospital, which was a couple of hours away. They had not travelled far when another call came through to say she had died. The blood they were waiting for had just arrived. It was a sad time. My Aunty had died after childbirth from loss of blood. The family received a sympathy card, and one on the front of the card was Psalm 23. I learnt it by heart. It was a Psalm that I would draw on many times in the future. My maternal grandmother also died during the time I was nursing as a teenager.

A Psalm of David

The Lord is my shepherd, I shall not want.
He makes me to lie down in green pastures.
He leads me beside still waters.
He restores my soul:
He leads me in the paths of righteousness for his names sake.
Yea, though I walk through the valley of the shadow of death,
I will fear no evil; for you are with me; your rod and your staff they comfort me.
You prepare a table before me in the presence of thy enemies;
You anoint my head with oil: my cup runs over.
Surely, goodness and mercy shall follow me all the days of my life:
And I will dwell in the house of the LORD forever.

-Psalm 23 (NKJV)

Although I had three close family members die while staying in the nurses' quarters, there was no offer of talking to anyone about things that happened. Nurses were meant to be tough. When we experienced the death of our patients, we were to show no feelings. Looking back I am not able to recall anyone speaking about a death of a patient. There was no support; it was like it didn't happen.

I had been nursing for three years, and during my annual holidays, I visited a special Aunty. It was a great time going to the beach, and having a barbecue, and roasting potatoes to go with the fish; we had green apples for dessert. I had completed three years of a four year course when I was asked to resign after failing an exam. I do recall a telephone call from Matron, one evening just before night shift. I was to do an exam the next morning before I left for holidays. The reason I was given to redo the exam was that the subject was changed to 70 percent to pass. I had not prepared for the exam, and at the end of seven weeks on nights I was feeling tired and looking forward to a break.

Luckily, I had always been a saver, and with what money I received, when I left work, I could go to the city to find another job. My mother travelled on the overnight train to the city with me. Fortunately, I had the name of an employment agency. After going went for an interview I got a position the first day. It was a live-in position so accommodation was catered for. At the end of the day, I went to live in the nurses' quarters, and my mother caught the train home in the evening.

I realised that I had lost all my confidence. My self-esteem was totally shattered. I was asked by the Matron if I wanted to complete my course. I didn't feel worthy of it so didn't even try. That is why now I tell myself, "If you don't try, you will always regret not giving it a go." I only stayed in the city for six months

My mother asked me if I would go home and mind the home while she had a holiday. A girlfriend came with me, and we shared the duties of opening and closing the railway gates. It was an experience for my friend, who was a city girl. She wanted her sister to see what we were doing in the country. Her sister and a couple of friends came to visit. They travelled on the night train and I recall how they had got off the train at the wrong stop. We received a telephone call and in the early hours of the morning to let us know where they were. Fortunately, we were able to get someone to take us to pick up our friends. When we arrived at the station, they were settling in for a sleep lying on the seats in the waiting room. This was their introduction to travelling by steam trains, and the pace of country life.

When I was preparing to go back to the city to find work, my father came home after they had been to visit family members. I was told that there was employment available, cooking in a hotel. My father drove me to the interview. I was able to start straight away; again I had accommodation with meals. The room I had at the hotel was near the kitchen so I didn't have far to go to work. I had always been able to get a live-in position up until this time. I realise that the positions I went for were usually ones where I had a roof over my head and food, so my basic needs would be met.

Before I started at my new place of work my girlfriend stayed a couple of extra days. We spent the time going into town, and to visit the shops so I could get a uniform, and shoes suitable for work.

CHAPTER 5
Education

As a child, I was taught to believe that education was important if you wanted a good job. I was also taught to believe if you use your skills and abilities, you could do anything. I spent a lot of time being an observer. I observed my mother as she used what she had to make things. You could make a meal out of what was in the cupboard and in the garden; there were no shops nearby. There was always flour and sugar, vegetables in the garden, and eggs in the henhouse. My mother would milk the cow, and then we would separate the milk and use the cream to make butter.

By the time I went to high school, I was competent to make dinner every night for a family of nine. I was able to make the staples last until the next delivery. If I wanted butter, I made it. My mother had shown me you could make clothes for the family by unpicking and remaking clothes into fashionable items. This included unpicking jumpers that were worn out. This process began by pulling the knitted item apart. The wool was put around the chair to straighten. The yarn would be washed, and made into a ball of wool before knitting a new garment. I was taught how to draft patterns to make my own clothes. If I was going out to a special event, I would make a new garment to wear.

At school, I was educated in home economics, which covered sewing, draft-making, and cooking. Cooking also covered how to wash stockings, woollens, and windows. Yes, they were practical classes in school where we became skilled with practice how to be a homemaker. My mother taught me how to manage with what I had and I heard her say many times "you can get by on the smell of an oily rag."

My mother taught me well by example how to get by on a very small amount, or an absolute minimum, which included money. Oh dear, the memories! I was taught to believe whatever happens in life, I could take stock, look at what I had, and work from there.

We were taught about time management and knew the time to be home on time. We knew if we weren't home on time, someone would have to come looking for us. Something may have happened to us. Looking back, that was understandable as we walked through the bush to school. With this background, we understood we needed to make sure someone would know where we were when we left the house, and what time we would be expected home. Dinner was on the table by 6.00 p.m.; and the whole family would be present. Once everyone was seated, we would say grace and serve the meal.

We didn't wear watches. The only thing outside the home we had to judge time was thc local mill whistle that rang at specific times 7.00 a.m., 1.00 p.m., and 4.00 p.m. We also knew the times the trains would come throughout the day.

I was also taught that one doesn't have to do what everyone else is doing. The mantra was to keep active. Mum sayings "Busy hands keep you out of trouble." "Don't come back home empty handed," and "Many hands make light work," were regular sayings. Even on our walk home from school, we had to pick up sticks along the way to use in lighting the fire.

Once we went to High School, our mode of transport was by bus. I come to know how to manage my time once I arrived home from school. My duties included changing from school clothes, to house clothes; preparing dinner having it on the table by 6 p.m. then and doing my homework. There were to be no excuses. Bed time was 9.00 p.m., for all the family. The year we got electricity was a highlight. I was able to keep the light on and complete my homework.

I believe that my mother didn't want her daughter's life to follow in her footsteps. Education and getting a job was a precursor for not getting pregnant, which appeared to be socially acceptable at this time. I recall girls who did fall pregnant during these years were often sent away to return without a child, or being rushed into marriage.

People who taught me about being educated included parents, teachers, Sunday school teacher and a neighbour. Observing the teachers on how to dress influenced me in the clothes that I wore then, in turn, the patterns I created for clothes I created. I was in my forties before I bought my own clothes. Previous to that, I had continued to sew clothing for myself and my daughters. Other people I observed during my childhood included my mother, who continued to keep busy by knitting, sewing, cooking, preserving fruit and vegetables, as well as making jam, sauces, and pickles. I was influenced by my father, who loved his garden and in his downtime loved to read.

I can thank my parents' belief was that girls were to get an education. My mother was saddened that she, being a second daughter did not have the same opportunity. It was a source of regret for her. Her older sister was able to attend high school. It was considered a privilege that I was sent to high school. My brothers were also less fortunate. They left school as soon as they were old enough to leave home and get a job. My brothers considered it was a grown-up thing to do. We grew up in a small country area we understood if we wanted to work, we would need to leave home.

CHAPTER 6
Meeting Future Husband

While working at the hotel as a cook, my job included being a housemaid and waitress. We had a wood-burning stove in the kitchen. Each morning, a man would come to clean out the ash from the day before. By the time I started my shift, the stove would be ready to cook breakfast for the workers who stayed at the hotel. The fire would be lit and wood place nearby to keep the fire going throughout the day. After using the stove for cooking, the top of the stove would be cleaned and polished by using a brush and wood stove black. It kept the stove looking clean and polished. My work colleagues included two sisters. We had lots of fun and enjoyed working together. At the end of our shift the publican would send in an orange juice for each of the staff. We were never offered alcohol.

Working as a cook allowed me to build on my skills in the kitchen. I loved cooking new things and organising the menu for the dining area. It was silver service. The cutlery was polished each day; the linen was starched and ironed. The table looked lovely with a crisp white tablecloth and serviettes. The table was set with the silverware and wine glasses. The furniture was polished each day ready for the patrons. Mostly the people who came to the restaurant were staying at the hotel accommodation. There were regular workers, who stayed during the week while working nearby.

On Saturday nights we would cook fish pieces at supper time for the patrons. I remember being told to put more salt in the food as it makes the patrons thirsty and they would buy more drinks. Some people would play indoor bowls.

I met my future husband while getting petrol at a service station. As we spent time talking we discovered that there was a connection with our fathers who had both worked in the timber industry. Sometime after this meeting I received a telephone call asking if I would like to go out to a dance. I could bring a girlfriend. I knew the place where he was going to take me as I had spent Saturday nights dancing there in the years I had been nursing. I had fond memories of the venue. Even though it was a hotel, I didn't drink alcohol. The great music and dancing was the reason the young people went there.

I was so shy and naïve. One time we went to a Chinese restaurant. I hadn't been to one before and did not know how to use chopsticks or what to ask for on the menu. It was so new to me, eating food that wasn't meat and three vegetables. I was feeling so uncomfortable sitting across the table talking during the meal, I asked him not to look at me. I felt so embarrassed, uncomfortable having a meal with him in such an intimate setting. Upon reflection I can see that I wasn't very confident at twenty years of age.

One night while travelling home, we had an accident. The car rolled over and went down an embankment on the side of the road. The driver had fallen asleep at the wheel, and as the car was veering over onto the edge of the road, I called out as we went into the ditch. My calling out shocked the driver and he pulled the steering wheel, and as it rolled I was trapped under the car until another car came and lifted the car so I could be pulled out. I was quite distressed, and no one was saying anything to me or asking me how I was. Although I had been helped from under the car, I felt alone as I struggled find the energy to climb the embankment to get onto the side of the road.

It was during this time I went to get my driver's licence. I was able to go to the police station where the local policeman took me out driving for the practical. He asked me lots of questions while driving. The road was very rough going through the local forestry. When we finished he said "If you can drive here you can drive anywhere". What a boost in confidence.

Once the holiday season at the hotel finished, I went to live in the town and worked at a local service station. This is where I gained knowledge of practical things like how to look after cars, checking the oil, tyres, battery and use the petrol bowser. Other duties included keeping the bookkeeping up to date; that was a short term position lasting three months.

I moved to a regional town looking for work. Fortunately, I was able to find work in a local factory.

This came about as I was walking along the street thinking to myself, *I'll need to go back home tomorrow* because my money was running out. I spoke to a lady who was down on her hands and knees washing the steps to the entrance of a hotel. As we talked, she told me that she heard about a place that was putting on staff. I got on a bus and went to the front gate. After speaking with security, I was sent to the personnel department. I started work the next day. This was factory work where I remained for three months. I don't think my mother liked me working in a factory. She asked me once again if I would mind the railway gates and look after the family while my parents went on holidays.

While I was at home, I was feeling quite safe, but t an experience happened that taught me how easily the consequence of gossip can affect another person. Sharing information was community news. Earlier that particular day I had a conversation with a person whom I hadn't seem for many years. We talked about general things including what was happening in our lives. I was home for a short time looking after family while my parents were away; they were expected back in a few days.

Retelling what was spoken would have been the highlight of the day. This incident taught me not to tell anyone what I was doing. I would feel uncomfortable if I heard people gossiping I would find myself wanting to walk away.

The same night after the earlier incident; the person who caused me so much grief came again. It was just before I turned twenty-one. He came during the night calling my name outside my bedroom window, I froze. Previously, he had sexually abused me as a nine year old, and returned when I was a teenager walking home after an evening with the fellowship group.

Fortunately, my parents had a change of plans. My parents came home earlier than expected. I believe that I was being looked after by something greater than the natural. This change of plans by my parents prevented anything happening the night the perpetrator had tried to make a house call. My father talking must have shocked the daylights out of him. My father called out "What are you doing here?"

However, my parents wanted me to stay in the district. My parents recognised who it was, and many years later, my mother kept telling what a nice person he was. At the time, I wanted to run from the district. I left the family home the next morning.

CHAPTER 7
Marriage

I moved to the city when I was twenty-one. I worked for a year before my future husband, asked me to marry him. There was a lot of pressure from the family as I was soon to be twenty two-years old and not married. Weighing it up and to please my family I decided to get married. I had no concerns about a future together. It was my understanding that we would continue to go to church with me each week. Our children would be brought up a Christians. During the time we were going out I had already taken his son to church to be confirmed in the church. The only concern was that my future husband had been married before. I felt under lot of pressure to get married. Somehow, I thought that the church wouldn't allow us to get married. My future husband had been divorced, but it wasn't long before we got a letter approving our forthcoming marriage in a cathedral.

To me marriage was meant to be a lifelong, monogamous relationship, both permanent and exclusive.

I soon discovered how naïve I was about life. I believed what I was being told about his first marriage.

I'd grown up with strong family values, and I went into marriage expecting to support each other in sickness and health, having children and to share our lives together. To be married, build a home together, and have children was my dream. The journey of life that I have lived wasn't the one I dreamed of as a young child. My parents were married for over fifty years. I was one of seven children and had seen many trials along the way with love seeing it through to the end and beyond.

Life changed from talking about having a life together, attending church together each week to, once married, I was told we didn't need to do that anymore. I believed that marriage was for life. I was brought up knowing that marriage was a sacrament, and it was important to me to keep that commitment. It wasn't until going through the divorce that the solicitor I went to was a Christian, and he said marriage is a contract. If one person breaks that contract, if it couldn't be renegotiated there is no contract. I had not heard the explanation before.

Once the wedding vows were said, red flags started flying. This is not what I expected to happen. At the reception, when my husband disappeared, it was one of my brothers who danced the bridal waltz with me. After changing into my going away outfit and returning with my bridesmaid to the reception room finding the room had been cleared and all the guests had left. My initial instinct was to run that day, but all my personal belongings were in the car; we had moved out of my accommodation that morning. We were moving to a regional town to begin our married life together. Regarding work, I had already requested a transfer to another area outside of the city. The transfer had come through, and I was due to start after the honeymoon, in six weeks' time. My husband said he had a new job to go to in a regional area after we were married. That information led me to request a transfer for work.

After we checked the venue and not finding anyone left in the reception hall we walked outside. I was surprised to find there were already six people in the car. I was told to get in the driver's side to slide across. My husband was the driver, leaving the total of eight people in the car. What a start to married life?

Starting married life was an interesting start to what the future would be. On the night we were married, my husband was to organise a place to stay. I have since heard that he was gambling on the day of the wedding; and continued betting while the reception was on. My parents gave us money for the wedding. Somehow history was repeating itself. The money was given to the man to pay for things. Gambling took it all. Therefore, the night we were married, we didn't have a place to stay. A friend from my workplace invited us to stay with them. All the guests had their accommodation organised. Once my mother-in-law heard we were staying in the city for the night, in the car my mother-in-law was heard saying that she would exchange her ticket for cash. Then she proceeded to tell us that we could drive her back home the next morning. Home was at least five hours away in the opposite direction of where we intended to travel for our honeymoon. I felt like I had no say in the decision.

I had no idea that our marriage would be such a lonely walk. Separate lives started on our wedding day. We did whatever his mother said. My mother-in-law was a forceful lady. I found out that she would pay the pawn brokers. She would look for the receipts for the goods her son had hocked before we were married. I was not prepared to continue doing this because it would enable my husband to continue with his gambling.

After six weeks, we had found a flat, and I started work at the Railways. I discovered that my husband didn't have a job. I felt duped. I was the one with permanent work. Being paid male wages and working shift work earned extra money. It didn't take long to realise how I was being used. I would keep a house, work and provide the perfect family look for my husband to continue life as a single person.

I became pregnant early in the marriage. I had morning sickness that lasted throughout my pregnancy. I took leave from work when I was five months along. I was given twelve months maternity leave. It was good to know that I had some sense of ownership in providing for my baby.

My mother made clothes and gave me three dozen cloth nappies for the baby. A cousin lent me a bassinet and a pram. I had the bassinet all set up and the pram was behind the door. When my husband came home and discovered that we had a second-hand bassinet and pram, he took the baby out of the bassinet. He then placed the baby on the bed. He took the basinet and the pram out of the house and put them in the boot of the car. He preferred me not to have anything than to have something second-hand - everything had to be new! Later, he returned the bassinet and pram to the person who had lent them to me. Leaving nowhere for the baby to sleep I took a drawer out of the dresser. I used a drawer and made a bed for the baby. I then placed the drawer on top of some boxes that were in the corner of the room. I wanted a pram as I did not have a car to be able to walk to the bus stop to do shopping. Money the government gave new mothers was enough to buy a pram.

I was constantly struggling to find enough money to buy adequate formula for the baby. I asked my workplace if I could go back to work early. After a medical this was approved.

I cannot recall anytime during this marriage when my husband would arrive home to sit down to a meal with the family. It was an expectation that I would have a hot meal on the table when he did arrive home no matter what time of the night. There was no apology or mention of where he had been only the strong smell of alcohol. On the outside, people would comment to me as to how generous he was. I was not given a regular amount to pay bills and every bit I did get I would be very frugal. I would go without things to keep the peace in the home. I was the one who answered the telephone, opened the door to the debt collectors who were asking for money. I would be told that I was his wife and I had to pay his debts as it affected my credit rating. I had the idea that I needed to save for item; if you can't pay for something, I wouldn't buy it. My husband would disappear for days at a time with no explanation about where he had been.

I had seen my mother being able to pay the bills. I also saw how frugal she was in budgeting. She showed me many ways that helped in saving money to pay the bills while saving for a rainy day. I was constantly challenged with organising the household so it would go as smoothly as possible while I was at work. For several months, I had a friend who offered to mind the baby. But when she broke her ankle and returned to her family, I was left without someone I could trust to mind my baby while I was at work.

At the end of the second year of our marriage, there were many changes. I continued to do shift work. My husband came home to tell me we were to move into a three bedroom home. I didn't know that it was planned as it would be in walking distance to where my stepson would go to high school.

During a weekend just before school began, I was told that a child from his previous marriage would be moving in with us to begin high school. There was no discussion about this change in family dynamics.

I discovered that the bags were already packed. I was working shift work, had a baby to look after, and now a teenager in the house. I was not yet twenty four years old and I being told that I was responsible for a teenager. It was overwhelming. By this time, my mother-in-law knew that her son was irresponsible, and would not come home to help. This was an extra burden on me as my husband wasn't about to change his ways.

I put an advertisement in the local paper to find a person who would mind my baby. Several people came to see about the job. Only one lady asked to see the baby. So she got the job minding my baby while I went to work. In the beginning she began by coming to the house to mind the baby. After some time it was decided that I would drop the baby off at her place on my way to work with the understanding that my husband would pick her up each evening.

One evening I arrived home from work around midnight. My baby wasn't there. I had no idea where my husband would be. I decided to drive where the babysitter lived. I noticed that her light was on, so I knocked on the door. As I gathered my baby and her things, she told me she wouldn't be minding the baby anymore. The next day, I was going on holidays, and I already had an envelope where I included holiday pay for her; my thinking was if I got paid for holidays, she needed to be paid as well. Before I went back to work, she came to see me and offered to look after the baby while I worked. I come to know while I was working in the evenings; my husband would have my baby in the car outside a hotel before picking me up from my workplace.

Changes in family dynamics changed again when I turned twenty eight. My stepson completed four years of high school and began his apprenticeship. My first child began school, and I gave birth to our second child. While I was pregnant with my second child my husband didn't want to know about the child. He kept accusing me, saying the baby wasn't his. I had morning sickness during the pregnancy I didn't have a lot of energy. I took maternity leave. Finances were short, and it was difficult to keep up with expenses. I suffered nutritionally as I fed everyone else before looking after my own health.

I had noticed my husband was buying new clothes, going to new places, and upgrading the alcohol beverages. Someone came to tell me he was seen driving around with another woman in the car. Whatever came over me when I got the strength to get dressed in my best maternity dress and putting makeup on and wearing stockings before getting into an old Ute to drive to where he had been seen. I walked into the venue, which I had heard that he frequented, and saw a couple sitting at a table. I realised that it was my husband with another woman. As I walked up to the table, I remained calm. I was so polite it would make anyone sick as I spoke calmly. I said goodnight to both of them. I quietly turned around and walked out of the restaurant. I was in shock going to the Ute. It was my way of letting them know, it couldn't be covered up anymore.

I was absolutely shattered and I felt that life was really the pits. I couldn't believe it - *he* had been claiming the baby wasn't his! He was telling other people I had another person in my life, while all the while, my husband was the one with another person in his life.

I had a friend who always seemed to turn up when my life was going pear-shaped. She was there when I returned back to the house. I remember the panic I felt at being pregnant. I was on leave from my work due to ill health and had no money. Things were constantly disappearing including food and money from the home. I couldn't see a way out. I felt totally devastated not knowing where to turn to or what to do. I had no income coming in and don't know how I'd survive.

The night our second daughter was born her father had been away for a couple of weeks. The contractions were getting closer, when he walked in the door just in time to drive me to the hospital. Husbands didn't stay with the wife back then. The nurse collected me at the door and told me to sit in a wheelchair, said goodnight to my husband before locking the doors and taking me to a ward. It all happened so fast.

CHAPTER 8
Reality Hits

I had no idea how bad things were. When the baby was a few months old, I answered the front door. A policeman was standing there with a gun drawn. At the back door was a policeman with a gun drawn. They asked to see my husband. As he walked out of the bedroom and went to the front door, the policeman placed handcuffs on his wrists. Without any explanation, my husband was taken away in a police car to the police station. I was overwhelmed by the chain of events.

It wasn't long before a couple turned up at the door saying that they saw my husband in the back of a police car. They were concerned about us and wanted to know if there was anything they could do for me. I was in shock, so the man went to the police station to ask what was happening and see if there was anything he could do for the family. I soon understood that the matter was serious, and the following day he would appear in front of a magistrate.

At the court proceedings, bail was set. I didn't have the money, so my husband was taken to prison to stay until his bail was paid or he had his court date. I felt a lot of pressure on me to fond the bail money. After speaking to my father about the situation, he went straight to the police station and out the family home up for bail. I was shocked that he would do that. It was the first time I had to go to try to get some assistance to buy food for the family. The person I saw said "I don't know why you women didn't put something aside for times like this". These comments have stuck in my mind and as soon as I could I would try to put money aside for at least three months housekeeping.

During the court case, it looked like it would be a term in prison. I was in court when I heard my husband say that we were moving to the city. He told the judge that his wife would be going back to work, so he would be able to pay the outstanding debt. This was the first time I had heard this. As I listened, I realised that my husband was talking about. The Judge would have seen the look on my face when my husband said with his wife working he would be able to pay the money that was owed. If the money owing wasn't paid, he would need to do time. I felt a lot of responsibility to ensure the money was paid back. This was all new to me, and I did not want to see my parents lose their home.

I felt like I was being manipulated, and I soon realised that I was being used again. My husband was expecting me to pay for his crime by going back to work. I felt so angry at the situation and feeling so guilty that this had involved my parents and their home. After weighing up the family situation, I went to the city with the family. I had made a decision it was his debt, and I would not be going back to work at that time.

Something snapped, and I made the decision to resign from my workplace and spend the time with my girls. Making a decision not to go back to work was easy. I realised from past behaviour that my working only gave excuses for my husband not to provide for us. I didn't have anyone who could help out with the children. Fortunately, I had a strong foundation to be practical. I could work things out and keep my faith. I would look for the positives in all situations; I didn't want to end up bitter.

After the court case was finalised, there were changes in the family dynamics. We moved, leaving the district and returning to the city. Our first accommodation was in a caravan park. This was a short stay until my husband found work. While looking for accommodation, we found a nice unit within walking distance of a school. I took the time to be a stay-at-home mother. It was my desire to spend time bringing up my girls.

I joined the Mothers' Club at the school to raise money for the school. I was asked at the annual general meeting if I would take the role of the president on the committee. I had no idea what that would entail, and I went to the library to get as much information as I could about running meetings. I decided that I would take the children to church and Sunday school. While I was in the service my children went to another area for Sunday school. I was happy being a mother to my two children without the pressure of going to work.

I knew that I could no longer trust my husband to come home after work when he said he would. I cannot remember one night when he came home to have dinner with us. I was often told I had a generous husband. They didn't know our circumstances in the home. They didn't seem to have any idea as to if a person who was married always had money for a social life that someone in the family would be missing out.

As I look back on my life it was the grounding I received as a young person, with the knowledge that nothing is wasted. We absorbed so much as our parents grew up in the Depression, those skills helped me get by; no matter what was happening. I could have a good life. I continued to make clothes and school uniforms as well as undo old jumpers using the wool to knit items of clothing. I am sure that I knew many ways to use mince and a side of lamb. Of course, my husband expected the best steak to eat for breakfast.

I certainly discovered that some people only tell you what they want you to hear. It all sounds so true; but it's simply to make them look good. It was always someone else's fault. Nothing changed, so I came to understand that I needed to get on with life and do it the best way I could.

When my younger child turned three, she started preschool. The manger suggested two days a week to see how my child would adjust. It wasn't long before the manager said "I think she needs more days" as she had been learning fast. This gave me the time to take an opportunity teaching the children religious education at school each week. I enjoyed working with the children.

I saw many opportunities open. I had given a lady at the school three uniforms, and one day I noticed that she kept looking at me. Finally, she came over and gave me enough money that I needed to buy groceries. This was definitely an answer to prayer.

Another opportunity opened when I had booked a live-in weekend course. I had no idea how I was going to pay for it. I had someone organised to stay with the children.

At the last minute I had a call to say it wasn't to start until the next day as the venue had double booked. That evening, a person turned up in time to give me the exact amount of money I was to pay for the weekend as the course was residential. I was able to help the family out previously and his wife asked him to come and give me an amount.

Another time, I was going to buy tickets for something for the children. I was waiting in line when a person came up to give me a cheque for something I had done for them. I could only think that God is good. It was like if you help people good things happen in unexpected ways. I did things not expecting anything in return.

I had stopped going over in my head about how I was being treated. I had peace in my life. I heard my husband say once that he couldn't work out what was happening to me.

Finances were short, but I needed to have some dental work done. I got a position to work one night a week. It was during this time that I had a miscarriage. I didn't know I was pregnant. Miscarriage was something no one wanted to talk about. I found it a difficult time emotionally. One evening, as I was about to go to work, my husband phoned. "You go to work. I'm on my way." I had to walk quite a distance, but when I got home the next morning, I learned that our children had been left alone all night. I knew that I should not have trusted him. Knowing I could no longer trust him to come home in time to mind the children, I felt that I had no choice but to resign.

I had been walking just outside of the front door. I was feeling like there was no hope when the words became like a beacon of light. "In my Father's house there are many mansions" (John 14:2 (NKJV). Somehow there seemed to be a promise of good things ahead as the Lord has gone before me and he has a place for me. I knew that I would find the words in the Bible. Somehow those words gave me a sense of hope and a change of attitude from feeling fear about my life to a sense of a knowing that my life would work out. I had this knowing that I would have a place to live no matter where life took me.

CHAPTER 9
Spine Surgery

In my early thirties, I had spine surgery after having a fall. After being in hospital for three weeks it was recommended that I have an operation on my spine. The first surgery I had was a Laminectomy on Lumber four and five to relieve the pressure causing numbness and pain. The hospital stay was six weeks.

While in the hospital the only book I had was the Bible. It was the book that my father gave me when I was ten years old. I carried it everywhere I went. I discovered through every death and resurrection experience there has been an answer in the Bible. My journey has been enhanced by my belief in Christ. I have met people who have come into my path who have given me answers and helped me on this journey.

On Sundays there was a Minister 'Robert Schuller" on the television that I had in my room at the hospital. He spoke of the possibility thinker's prayer. I got a copy and kept saying it each morning.

Possibility Thinkers' Prayer

When faced with a mountain I WILL NOT QUIT!
I will keep on striving until I climb over,
Find a pass through, tunnel underneath –
Or simply stay and turn the mountain into a gold mine,
with God's help!

-Robert Schuller

I continued to pray for healing. The pain was intense. I started praying the Lord's Prayer and saying the Psalm 23, that I heard when I was eighteen after the death of my Aunty. During the stay in hospital I had an amazing experience. While children were visiting a patient in the next bed they decided to play under my bed. With the bed being shaken, the pain became unbearable. During this time of severe pain, I had what I have ascertained that is what is called a born-again experience. I saw a white light and was drawn towards it. As I thought of my two beautiful daughters I felt this immense peace come over me, and I knew it would all work out for good. It became very clear that there was a reason to be alive. I stayed in the presence of this peace. I felt all the stress leaving my body; I had a knowing that I would be alright. I felt a faith that I had not felt in the past. I had a sense that I would be alright, expecting to walk out of the hospital.

I sensed that the answers would be found in the Bible. I recall the faith that I felt, and it was as it has been said: the old had gone, and the there was a new beginning. Without knowing that God loves me and His Word to stand on, I could not begin to imagine where I would have been today. I praise God for the journey of life that has brought me to where I am today.

Although I had severe pain from the spinal surgery, due to life circumstance I decided not to take anything for the pain once I left the hospital. As I continued to pray for my physical healing I found the past began coming back to haunt me. The traumas of the past were being brought into light, and I began to experience the pain and the emotions of events that were long buried. As I was dealing with issues from the past I was getting mentally and physically stronger.

It was during this time I began to understand how words spoken can have an effect on a person while going through the valleys. Some words can be devastating and cause more guilt and pain. Other words can be uplifting and with support can take us to the mountain-tops. I realised my hope was in knowing Christ as my Lord and Saviour. There have been quiet times where I have been able to take the time to reflect.

I have come to know how to bloom where I am planted. My faith was strong and I had a knowing that I would find the answers to my problems in the Bible. I had the Bible in the drawer beside me. I have to say I had not opened it very much before this time. I was alone in the hospital without any visitors. I had no idea what was happening at home.

What a shock I had when I went home in an ambulance and was taken on a stretcher to the upstairs unit that we lived in. I had been fitted with a brace that I was to put on before I got out of bed. I was told not to sit. Only stand up and lay down. When I went back to the surgeon for the follow-up an Ambulance came to get me and bring me back home. There was no rehabilitation and I came to know how to do things around the home. What helped me was listening to the *Hour of Power* on a Sunday morning. I recall one message spoke of needing to crawl before you can walk. That stirred me on to watch how my younger child had been learning to walk and go up and down the stairs. So to strengthen my legs, I would walk holding the railings out on the balcony. While going up and down the stairs, I would take a step one at a time until eventually I was able to go up and down the stairs with ease. I found that I could pick up things with my toes and place items on a lounge. As soon as I was able to do more things I lost that ability.

Once I felt strong enough to attend church I would walk to the bus and stand the entire drive. I would stand at the back of the church, and when the service finished, the children and I would walk to the bus stop to return home.

As soon as I could drive again, I drove to church. I recall building my strength to drive I would go to start the car, driving down the driveway until I would be able to drive the car down the street. I had a friend who would telephone me every morning after her children left for school. We would talk - or more to the point, I did a lot of listening for at least an hour each morning. Eventually when I was confident enough I would say, "I'm going to drive to your place." I would drive to her place. After a period of time, we would go to the supermarket to do shopping. I would push the trolley while she got the items off the shelves. Our outings included putting the groceries in the boot of the car. When we had finished all of our shopping we would take all my groceries upstairs, before I would drive to her home. To help out, I paid for the petrol for the car and my friend would buy magazines and she would pass them on to me when she had finished. Our shopping experience may have taken longer but it felt like together we accomplished something worthwhile. A problem shared is a problem halved. We were always able to make fun of what we were doing.

During this time, my husband would come home and would tell me about a church across the road from his workplace. It appeared to be a friendly group of people, and the minister spent time talking to the parishioners. One morning as I was driving down the street to make a right turn to go to my regular church I drove left. This road took me to the church opposite where my husband was working. When I walked into the church I felt that I was at home.

There was a person speaking about needing a Scripture teacher at the local school. When I spoke to my husband about it he supported my studies and teaching scripture at the local school; and encouraged our daughters to attend church with me. During this time my husband continued drinking and gambling. The children enjoyed going to Sunday school. I got involved with the women's' group and youth group.

CHAPTER 10

Feeling Isolation and Rejection

I discovered that isolation and rejection comes with the shame of events that happen along the way. I also come to know it is not always what we had done but the effect of what others have done that affected my sense of calm.

Choices I make and others make can have consequences that affect other people. . Choices that are made by others can also affect our lives can be life-changing. A decision that is made can change the direction of our lives. This defining moment can also come as a result of someone else's choice, that choice at times affected our lives as a family. Family and friends often reject them. Because of this ordeal we may feel abandoned or rejected by the significant others in our lives. In my time of need where I expected support I found that I was shunned. Family and friends didn't know what to do. They just stayed away.

Looking back I realised that they did not know what to do. There is no one to blame for not being there.

Often I didn't know what to do when I found myself in the middle of a crisis. I found that friends and family were very judgemental looking for someone to blame. There were the friends I met with each week. We had been like-minded people until I opened up about my life and challenges I had been facing.

At a group I attended each week, instead of supporting me, were great at giving their insights as to what was wrong with me. They spent their time telling me I was the problem because of the situation. I must be doing something wrong. I must have had an issue that I hadn't dealt with that caused the problem in the family.

At the time, I felt the finger was pointed at me because of the silence. What was happening was confusing when I was being told by family members "You should go to work to give him money; that way he wouldn't have to do the things he did". I had two young children and their needs were not even considered while placing blame on me.

Sometimes when we feel rejected, we can even reject people who actually want to support us in our time of need. This support can come in an unexpected way. I met one person who listened and supported me. She became a friend indeed. She showed no rejection in our conversations, no blame was laid. These friends are special. Everyone needs one like that.

The crisis showed me my real friends, or at least the ones who could be nonjudgmental. I didn't have the energy to keep trying with friends who were not helpful. It wasn't helpful to me to get into conversations with people, who implied that the problem was caused by me. It used up too much energy and it didn't help my self-esteem.

I could have chosen to isolate myself, but instead, I worked out quickly who I could trust and who was non-judgmental and spent my energies with them. Shock of hearing about a loved one who is in trouble with the law is life shattering. It is a time of re-evaluating our own lives and making choices. It can give us an opportunity to make good decisions or we can withdraw from life.

This experience can affect how we see God. I found the situation brought me closer to God. I may have been rejected from my friends with their judgements, but it took me on a path that brought me closer to God with an understanding of His love and mercy. From my experience I would see a 'back door' when we had a crisis as a family. I found that prayers and a quick telephone could be helpful. However, I wanted to be with a group of people that understood.

I got the courage to change. I went to see a counsellor about my situation, but I did not feel as though I was being heard. After a few months, I telephoned and spoke to a lady who gave me an appointment time. When the consultation ended, she said there was a meeting being held in the building, and asked if I would like to attend. After listening to the group I felt that this is where I was at. I felt that I had a place where I could open up and get some clarity.

I finally found a support group that would understand. Sometimes I went to five meetings a week.

The anonymity of the group allowed people to be themselves without judgement. "What you see here; when you leave here; let it stay here" were words that were encouraging to hear to be able to share my story. I found that situations that affected me in my life were crashing down on me. I felt so alone. Alanon family group gave me an opportunity to share my experiences, strength and hopes, in order to solve common problems. What interested me was it had no affiliation with organisations and had one purpose was to help families. The person who had gone before me was able to tell their story. When possibly when the time was right could be something that I could draw on.

The Serenity Prayer

God grant me the serenity
To accept the things I cannot change,
Courage to change the things I can,
And wisdom to know the difference.
-Reinhold Niebuhr

I realised that I needed to count one day at a time, and sometimes it was one minute at a time. Putting first things first, let go, and let God take over as a person made his or her own choices. I discovered how to keep an open mind in whatever the circumstances, count my blessings, and any change to let it begin with me. I could do this by asking myself, “How important is it?” I learnt to think and say, “But for the Grace of God." (John Bradford, circa 1510-1555).

I built my self-esteem to where I could say things as they were, be heard without judgement, and find in that process I was able to process my feelings and look at the situation differently. I became aware that rejection that comes through a crisis in our lives could strengthen us if we chose to deal with it in a constructive way, instead of isolating ourselves. My self-esteem had grown since I understand the power of positive response to rejection to move forward. When a family crisis happens and I feel alone in the midst of it, I have come to know that I needed to find a group of like-minded people.

CHAPTER 11
Impact of Divorce

When my husband left the marital home, he did not say anything. I was out with the children, and when arrived home, he had moved out. The house felt like something was wrong when I walked into our bedroom. As I opened his wardrobe, I saw that all his things had been taken. I also noticed at the time my girls were acting strangely, as though they knew something but didn't want to tell me. I heard many years later that he had told the girls he would be leaving.

I had been working a few hours a week as a volunteer at the school canteen. I knew that I would need extra income to keep the family together. As I was being driven home after finishing at the canteen, the driver said to me that she had been a sole parent. She advised me to go to social security to get some help. It didn't sit well with me. However, I did go, and started to get some assistance. Budgeting was something that I did well, and whatever help I received the money would be mine and I could make it work. In fact, having money of my own was empowering, I held the purse strings. I felt energised and even had a budget for saving for a rainy day and holidays.

I was accepted to do a counselling course. I didn't have the money to continue with study, so I went to an employment Agency to see if I could get some help to study. At the interview, I was told they couldn't help with the payment to study. Afterwards, there was much discussion as to what I had been doing as a volunteer and the skills I had acquired. Through experience being secretary then president of a club. I spoke about how I'd been to the library to find books on how to do these positions effectively. One of the issues we had looked into was the need for child care after a little boy died after being left home alone while his parents worked.

The voluntary work gave me the stepping stones to getting work. I decided to listen to my inner voice to go to visit the employment agency. I was forty years old and was told that I was a woman and wouldn't get a job, I was also told that I was too old to work. I decided that wasn't what I thought of my future. I went with trepidation as I had heard volunteer work would not get you a job. I discovered that volunteer work will give you skills that are transferable to the workplace. That morning a position came available for a sole parent to do a fifty two week employment program. I was offered a position that was available. They wanted someone to help with looking at the needs of childcare in the organisation. Fortunately this was one of the issues that I had been part of with the parents group at a school. Another time, I felt that I was to take the next step and not listen to people around me.

I was offered a position in a department where I was in a position to accept further training. My understanding today had a beginning in changes in the diversity of the workplace. Equal Employment Opportunity training in the workplace for women included 'Training in Assertiveness" so women could have a voice. One of the documentary films we watched was called *Lousy Little Sixpence,* which related to the amount of money that Aboriginal children were to be paid for their forced labour. It gave us an insight into the stolen generation and the struggles Aboriginal people had with the Australian Protection Board. Diversity in the workplace included gender, race, age, ethnicity, sexual orientation and religion. I had been away from the workplace for twelve years there were many changes. I saw many changes for the better for women. My biggest culture shock was calling your manager by their first name. It was so new to me coming from a formal communication style to our elders.

As a woman and a sole parent, I got an amazing opportunity to go back to work when it was frowned up. It changed my life. As a woman I had lived through many changes in the workplace.

Being part of the beginning of Equal Employment Opportunity (EEO) in the workplace in Australia was life-changing. I recall in the 1960s women who got married in many government positions had to leave work.

Life sometimes gives us the people who we need to say words that stay with us. I met a person who kept saying "You can do it, have a go". I discovered being a woman didn't stop me from finding employment. I went back to work at a time when I was forty and heard a lot of negativity in particular I was too old and you are taking a job from a younger person.

Sometimes I just made the best of whatever situation I was in, whether it was finding employment, having to relocate to a new city, starting a new life in a community, being divorced, a sole parent or widowed.

I have discovered if something needs to be changed I need to speak about it knowing that nothing that happened in my life was wasted. Each event and the lessons I come to know has been something that I could draw.

After I started working at the age of forty, I decided to do volunteer work as a telephone counsellor. I mentioned it to a parent from the local school. It was a Saturday afternoon when I received a telephone call at home, and I soon realised there was something wrong. Listening skills were suddenly important-not just the words but what was behind the words. I was able to keep her talking to find out where she was, and sent my daughter to get a neighbour to telephone the ambulance.

Once the ambulance got there and spoke to me, the call ended. This was first time I had an experience with a suicide in progress.

I can recall asking the question "What about the family?" They are shattered by this experience but are expected to live life as normal. In reality life is not the same again. How do you help a person who considers taking their life?

While working, I was encouraged to take tests for public service. After ten months, I was offered a full time position with another organisation. After being there awhile I was asked to apply for the position of welfare officer. This again came out of my voluntary work and the skills I had acquired. As I had already been doing volunteer work as a telephone counsellor and helped set up a care centre I felt equipped to try out for the position.

CHAPTER 12

Second Marriage

I met my second husband while we were attending the same church. However, when it came to getting married, he wanted to be married in the church that he went to as a young child.

Again marriage change things. My husband had been caring, doing home renovations, took over the kitchen, something I had loved to do. But he had the evening meal cooked each evening when I came home from work. I was suddenly being told that I was to attend the church where we were married, and he would continue to go to the one where we met. I was in shock about the change in behaviour. When it came to social outings, I was told we were married but he would go on his own.

After a short time, I noticed that my husband began to limp. I asked him to go and see a Doctor. After he saw a doctor, he began to act differently toward me and refused to tell me about what happened at the doctor's. From that day, he withdrew and did not talk about personal things.

Suddenly without warning after visiting his friend, my husband said that he had made a decision that he was leaving the marriage, and moved out of the home. There was no satisfactory explanation.

After we separated, we met in the same social environment each week and continued to be friendly toward each other. It was a shock when he spoke of divorce. That was final. We had been married two years when the divorce made the end of the marriage final. Several years later, I received a telephone call to let me know that he had died and I was invited to attend a memorial service for him. I heard that the cause of death was bone cancer.

CHAPTER 13
Third Marriage

I met my third husband while attending a training course for crisis counselling. The first-hand experience of a friend who called after taking an overdose of pills sent me on a journey of finding out as much as I could about suicide prevention. At the time I had no idea that this training would be helping me in my life experience.

I met my third husband while we were both attending a training course for telephone crisis counselling. We were married the following year. We had some great times travelling and even travelled to England the following year. I enjoyed seeing Liverpool in the United Kingdom through his eyes. We also discovered the place where my own grandfather was born. At home, we tried to get our own traditions with a blended family. My husband was diagnosed with a mental illness after attempting suicide three and a half years later.

A day that is imprinted on my mind forever began on a beautiful sunny day. It was Easter Monday in the year 1993. We were going to have lunch with friends. My husband took my car out of the garage and said "You go; I'll stay home and get some work done." During this time my husband was concerned about retrenchment. He had been told he would need to reapply for his position and was doing a course at University. He hadn't done any study since he was in school. As I drove away, I felt a sense of doom. The only indication there was a problem was the way my husband spoke. It was the first time he didn't want to go with me. We did everything together.

When I got to our friends place I asked to use their telephone to call a member of the family to ask if he could go and see my husband while I was out. I was concerned about the change in his demeanour. I decided to go back home only to find that no one was home. After some time, I decided to phone a family member, who proceeded to tell me two members of his family went to our home and taken him to a local hospital. What they found was a suicide in progress in the garage, and had taken to the hospital without calling an ambulance. It wasn't what I expected to hear.

This was my first experience of an attempted suicide by a loved one and I was devastated. The car still had the hose attached in the garage. Nothing prepared me for this. I believe having some training helped in keeping my husband alive for a long time as there were many tough times.

I did telephone some friends and when they arrived they began questioning me and wanting to know "What did you fight about?" The blame game began. No one wanted to remove the hose for me; I was left to do that. The hospital was saying that I was to take him home. I was trying to get my head around all of this.

My husband refused to leave the hospital. The hospital was adamant, saying it was twenty four hours after suicide attempt, and they could not keep him. All I could see was that the car still had the hose attached in the garage. I was being told we had to leave. We were paying into medical insurance. I persevered, and finally was able to get a bed in a psychiatric hospital. The same people at the hospital telling me earlier in the day that "He doesn't want to see you" and were now telling me I had to drive him to the psychiatric hospital. There was no offer of help from the family or friends and while quite traumatised by this I had to drive him. Not a wise move. But where was the help for a family in crisis?

We discovered quickly how the mental health system worked. After an attempted suicide a person can only stay in care for twenty-four hours.

I went home to remove the hose from the car myself. I was in shock. At the hospital, there was no support for the family. I was not told anything. It was confidential. It was his health and as his wife I couldn't get any information. I wasn't told of his medications or how to help with the health problem.

As a welfare officer I had no problem getting help from a medical person for a client. I understood I could get the help where the family couldn't. But as a wife, I had no voice. It appeared the mental health system did not know how to help the family during this traumatic time.

We were going through a dark tunnel. It was a lonely experience.

During this time a person I had known since I was twenty turned up at my house, saying that her daughter was in a psychiatric hospital the same time my husband was in hospital. We supported each other for many years. She became my McDonalds friend. I come to know talking to another person going through a similar experience is very powerful in recovery. The person understands that this is not a normal medical condition and the person closest was being treated as the enemy to the patient.

I quickly discovered there are some events are just not talked about. Some topics are difficult to discuss as every member of the family and friends are all seeing and being told something different. Talking about the grief for the family after an attempted suicide is just as taboo. Looking back, bereavement started after the first time my husband attempted suicide. This grief was devastating. There is a loss of the marriage as we knew it. But there was also hope for the future. That life would get better.

CHAPTER 14
Chronic Fatigue Syndrome

While I was visiting a church I met a lady who reminded me that she had met me twenty years earlier. She reminded me as to how ill I had been during this time. In the midst of my husband's illness I became ill. I was diagnosed with having Chronic Fatigue Syndrome many months after falling ill with a virus. I am not sure now whether it was a virus as I still find perfumes and chemical can take me on a downhill spiral if I do not remove myself from that environment. I had been attending a five day course, and there was a person in the room who wore an extremely powerful perfume. I found it overwhelming. Each day I was becoming unwell, by the end of the week I found it difficult to get myself home from work. I telephoned my husband to come to take me home. As soon as I walked in the door I got myself on the bed.

The following morning, I discovered that I could not move my body to lift my arm or hand to move the sheet off me to get up. I remained in bed for months. I had extreme fatigue and at times was not able to do anything for myself. It wasn't anything like working hard and being tired at the end of the day. I found attempting to walk the muscles would be burning it was like hiking up the side of a mountain. The fatigue was not the kind of tired feeling that would go away after having a rest. Instead it would last a long time and would limit my ability to do ordinary daily chores.

I saw many medical professionals I was sent to see an oncologist. After doing checks, she suggested I make an appointment to see a Medical Specialist who had been doing research in this illness. After the results came back, and ruling out any other diseases with similar symptoms, I was diagnosed with Chronic Fatigue Syndrome. My own medical doctor didn't accept this diagnosis and sent me to another medical specialist to get a second opinion. He also said it was Chronic Fatigue Syndrome. I do remember walking out of the build and feeling really angry. To finally get a diagnosis after so many tests and visits to medical professionals was a turning point. I turned the anger into energy to do my own research. This wasn't going to beat me. I would have a good life, just differently. I was open to new ideas.

With two separate diagnoses that supported CFS, my own medical doctor sent me to see a psychiatrist. After our initial interview, he said, "Return in a month I will do some research." When I returned for my next visit the Psychiatrist told me that I didn't need to see him; I needed to see an occupational therapist. It helped so much. I was shown how to put items that were used all the time at bench level so I didn't use energy to reach up. Every action I did would use energy. I would have no reserves left to complete any tasks. I had a friend come each week to do the house cleaning. She was my only social interaction outside of the home.

We tried many things to help, including diet and eliminating perfumes and chemicals. I travelled in the hospital bus that would pick me up and bring me home each time I attended the support group. Being part of a group was helpful listening to the group members share how they were doing things differently and how they were learning to adjust to this condition. I discovered that the brain is also a muscle, and it was to be respected like any muscle in the body. At least in a group, we understood about having to make notes all the time about anything. There were many times we laughed so hard because we would understand and we were making light of things we couldn't say outside the group. There were many challenges, but with support of the group, we were able to share things and hear that each person who had the illness had different unexplained symptoms. I would leave the group with energy to keep looking towards a brighter future.

I come to know about a program from an article that a colleague had sent me. I was able to get the details of the program as it was to be done. It worked for me as two days after starting the program my head cleared for me to finish a puzzle that I was going to finish one day. Then I began to walk short distances around the home.

I was called for jury duty that I insisted on going to. I knew it was something to do to be part of the justice system. My thoughts were that it would be interesting and a rewarding experience. The case went for three days. I got my husband to take me each day. After I realised I could retain the evidence put forward in the court I made a decision about going back to work. My future was looking brighter.

I made an appointment to see about rehabilitation to get back to work. I was trying to work out how much I could do each day. The physiotherapist would meet me at a heated pool twice a week. She arranged for a taxi to take me to the pool. Little by little, my confidence and the strength in my muscles came back. I started going to work for three hours at a time, three days a week. A taxi was arranged to pick me up and bring me home from work.

I began to understand how to manage my energies. I became aware that if I put energy in the bank today I could do more things tomorrow. If I was going out tomorrow I needed to have a quiet day today. It is like putting money in the bank to be able to buy something you need. Today, I still have awareness what will affect my body. In particular perfumes and chemicals can drain me of energy. I have gained knowledge of what I need to do such as changing my environment, moving away from the situation and getting some clean air and drinking lots of water. I have understood how to manage the symptoms to have a good life. My health was improving. I was back at work full time, Joseph was working. Things started to look up again.

I became aware that I needed to go to bed at the same time each day, and I avoid daytime napping, although I do have quiet spaces throughout the day. I limit my activity even on good days. I keep a diary, checking it regularly when I'm asked to do something I know my limitations and at times have suggested when another time would suit me better. I began to understand if I didn't pace myself, I could have more days when I am limited as my energy level is low. Also I am open to seeing a psychologist or attend a group to look after my mental welfare. It is looking after both my physical and mental health that continues to give me a good life that I experience today.

CHAPTER 15
Changes

Toward the end of 1995, we went to the United Kingdom to attend a wedding. At the last minute my mother-in-law mentioned an aunt was not well and would like to go and visit her. We made a decision to take his mother with us. On our return, Joseph went into a spiral with his mental health. Two months later, an incident happened that showed me first hand that homicide suicide was also very real.

On Christmas Eve, I arrived home from work and he said "Let's go up to your mother's for Christmas Day." Joseph was saying that he didn't want to see his family during Christmas. Looking back, that was a warning sign as he had always wanted to be with his family on Christmas Day. As we were travelling up the coast an episode happened that showed me how easy it would be for people to think it was a road accident when it would have been homicide and suicide.

I believe my awareness and crisis training kept us both alive. The incident happened before we had mobile telephones. I had no way of letting anyone know what was happening. I recall thinking "*I need to leave a note*" but I knew it wasn't safe to get a pen and paper out of my purse to write a note to leave to be found if I didn't make it. Much prayer and focusing on the scripture, "Be still and know that I am God" -Psalm 46:10 (NKJV), and told myself *don't react. Stay still*, while I was sitting quietly and not saying anything in the car.

When we got to a town, my husband wanted some money. I told him that I didn't have any cash and would need to go to the ATM. He held onto my purse, and I only had the card. I got some money out and didn't know what to do. I got back in the car, and while he took the money he handed me my handbag. I had a split second to get out of the car. He drove the car on the footpath to try and run me down. There had been no arguments, just a change in his demeanour. A couple who appeared from nowhere helped me, and they called the police. While my husband drove back home; the police said it was just a domestic incident. It was Christmas Eve; I was in a refuge four hours away from home. I just prayed that Joseph would stay safe. On reflection, I accept that he had planned to take us both out.

When I came back home Joseph was sitting on the back steps. He said, "Don't tell anyone; if you do I will burn the house down." He got my car out of the garage. "I want you to leave." I told him where I would go to stay giving him the telephone number where I would be staying. I didn't know what to do but to stay safe. The police said it was a domestic, the Psychiatrist didn't believe he would try to take his life but proceeded to tell me to "Stay safe".

On arrival at my friends place, I was surprised them waiting for me. They came out of the house and spoke to me as I pulled into their driveway. They said that I was wanted on the telephone. I picked up the phone and my husband was telling me "The fire brigade is here." What I didn't know until later one of his children had turned up. After a conversation in the front of the house, he told them he was on his way out. I later he mentioned he thought I had told his family that he wasn't well; he went back inside and put a pan of oil on the stove to get the fire started before leaving to go to the local post office to collect mail from the post box. He tried to burn the house down.

Fortunately, we were in a private health fund so there was no problem in getting hospitalised when my husband requested it. As a wife, I couldn't get the help. The person who was in an episode I was told that "Joseph had to ask for help." In contrast, I recall thinking if he had a heart attack he would have had medical treatment. I would have had some input in knowing what was going on.

The signs were there. Each episode got more serious and methods changed.

CHAPTER 16

Return to Study

After seeing the deterioration of Joseph's health, my concern for his condition grew. At work, leave was cancelled for everyone, this particular day I had this sense to ask if I could have a week off. When I put the leave form in and it was approved, I felt a real excitement in my spirit.

I had mentioned to a person from the church that I had the next week off; that I knew there was some reason but had no idea why. This is when I heard about a conference the following week. After getting directions to go to the booking office, I went along to see if I could get a ticket. It was supposed to have been sold out. On the way, I telephoned a friend from church. Although neither of us had the money, we believed if it was meant to be, we would be able to attend. Later that year, I made a decision to do further study. When I went for the interview before commencing the following year, a comment was said. "Yet who knows whether you have come to the kingdom for such a time as this?" (Esther 4:14 (NKJV). My reality was that the experience of crisis was happening, and God would use while it was happening, through the experience and after the experience ended.

At my workplace, I was able to take my long service at half pay. By the end of that year, I was able to retire from work, taking a part pension for income. By this time, the decision was easy as my husband's health was deteriorating. It was at the end of that year, just before second year and graduation my husband died by suicide.

CHAPTER 17
Mental Illness

A diagnosis of a mental illness of a loved one gives a family so much unspoken trauma along the way. When the illness was stable, Joseph was the husband I married but when he went off his medication life was very different. The signs were there as Joseph had made previous attempts to take his life. At times, Joseph just wanted to live in isolation. I would come home from work to find Joseph was still in bed. At times I could not motivate Joseph to do anything. During those times, that I was left to do everything including encouraging him to change his clothes, bathe, eat as well as take his medication. Looking back, I can pinpoint the day he had already made a decision to end his life. I could not find any medication in the house, knowing that I had just got his prescriptions made up for him.

Typically, his attitude and behaviour was so out of character that it was a shock to watch a man who had such a high moral character change. His last episode lasted several weeks. It was as if no one was going to change his mind. He resented me trying to get him help, and he turned against me. Life was not easy. He told me to act as if I didn't live there so he could bring other women into the home. I spoke to his psychiatrist, and he said, "You need to need to go home and check on him". This particular time, I took two co-workers with me that I was working with. On the lounge were two people. I didn't recognise Joseph at first as he changed so much depending on where he was in the episodes. I said "I am his wife." The lady left. The man who came with me spoke to Joseph and when we were leaving the home said "He is convincing." I was told by a neighbour that they had arrived home just before I did. Joseph later told me that he had met her at a coffee shop and asked to come to the home. It was at that time I saw a wardrobe moved out form the wall in a bedroom. When I checked, the ceiling had been removed and a rafter was exposed. He began to give possessions away, both his and mine.

One day, I came home found that he had divided up the house. The blinds were torn down, and there were no curtains hanging. He would at times have a change of mood toward me. It was during these episodes that I knew to keep myself safe. I was in shock not knowing what the next step would be. No one would hear my cry. I went to many people for help. His previous medical history did not appear to mean anything.

Living with a person who had a mental illness was devastating, but with suicide there is no more hope for a relationship with the other person. I have felt shock, hurt, confusion, loneliness and rejection. No one told me how much worse it could be when the person actually succeeds in taking his life. No words can describe the devastating pain and emotions I experienced during this time.

It was a nightmare during the months leading up to the time Joseph was missing. There were many who did not want to accept that he had an illness. This road we travelled in most part alone from the time Joseph was diagnosed with a reactive depression. Leading up to this episode, my husband's workplace was going through organisational change; and he had a fear of being retrenched as well as needing to reapply for his position in the workplace. It was overwhelming with too many changes were happening at the same time. He began to study forty years after leaving school. Three years later he was diagnosed with Bipolar Disorder. Six and a half years after it was diagnosed with reactive depression Joseph died. The years were challenging to say the least. I felt so alone going through the trauma leading up to Joseph's death.

In the week before Joseph went missing, he finally booked into a hospital. He knew that I had been planning a family gathering four hours away. After Joseph went to hospital I went to stay with my daughter overnight. The plan was to leave the first thing the following morning. As I was driving out of the city, I had a sense of needing to return to our home first. As I walked inside the house, I saw the light flashing on the answering machine. On checking the messages, I heard my husband's voice saying that he was in trouble; and was going up the coast to the next state where his mother lived. I checked with the hospital where he had gone to. I was told Joseph had signed himself out the previous evening. As a wife, I didn't get a courtesy call from the staff at the hospital to let me know. The hospital was telling me it was confidential; they could not tell me anything further. Joseph wasn't answering the mobile.

This had happened before, and as a wife I found that my side of things was not taken seriously. I let some of his family know and set off to see if I could find joseph. I felt so alone driving up the coast, checking all the side roads. I telephoned people I knew if they would check side roads for me. Later in the day I called in to have something to eat at my parent's home. Before I left to continue up the coast I telephoned a member of his family. I was told he had been found in a room at a motel and been taken to a public hospital. Staff at the hospital told me that they could only keep him for twenty four hours; I would need to come and pick him up the following morning. I stayed the night with my mother about two hours away.

Joseph's car was left outside a police station. The keys were at the front desk. They had no concern about handing the keys over to Joseph. There nothing I could do and legally I had no rights. A wife with no rights!

As usual Joseph was saying all the right things when I arrived at the hospital. I had already been told that they could not keep him there. As we had two cars Joseph insisted on driving himself back to my mother's home. On the way we stopped at a service centre to have coffee and something to eat. When we sat at the table Joseph read a Scripture "The eternal God is your refuge, and underneath are the everlasting arms; He will thrust out the enemy from before you, And will say, 'Destroy!'" (Deuteronomy 33:27 (NKJV)

When Joseph was ill, he wrote lists of things to do. This day was no different. He had his mobile telephone out and began making telephone calls. One of the things that he did was to set up an appointment with a psychologist for both of us on the following Monday. He was saying we need to have marriage counselling. It wasn't sitting right for me, but I agreed with making the appointment as I already knew that Joseph was not in a good space mentally. He gave me a list of where things were and telephone calls to make for him.

When we arrived at my mother's home, Joseph had lunch and wanted to have a sleep. He had left a message to speak to his psychiatrist. When the telephone call was returned the psychiatrist spoke to Joseph about returning to the hospital in the city as he has kept the bed for him. I felt like I had no support as the psychiatrist knew that I had arranged a family gathering. I would not be going back to the city that day but would be able go back the following afternoon after lunch.

When I telephoned the hospital later that evening I was informed that he had not returned to the hospital. I telephoned the police, and they told me they couldn't do anything until he was missing for twenty four hours. The next day, I left the lunch and telephoned the police to report that Joseph was missing.

The following morning, I woke early and went to place where we had spent time stopping for a cuppa in a bushland setting. I waited till 8.00 a.m. to speak to the police; it was a one-man station. As I began talking to the policeman, he picked up his sheet from the evening before, telling me that he had seen the car the previous evening. Joseph had been the second person that he pulled over for the breathalyser. I mentioned to the policeman that I had been checking roads. I gave him some places where I hadn't checked. I mentioned a road into the mountain nearby that Joseph had always talked about going up. Somehow an hour had been unaccounted for but he said this man was going north.

I drove back to the city, but I had planned to go back up the coast two days later. I got three photographs to give to the police. One was of the car and two of Joseph at different stages of his illness. I was aware of the changes in his behaviour and dress. On the fourth morning after Joseph was missing I gave the photographs to the police.

It was five days later when a photograph of the car was shown on the local television station that brought a result. A bushwalker came forward that had seen the car in a forest near where Joseph was last seen. He was found up the side of the mountain. The car was found parked in a quarry before walking further up the mountain to the place where he took his life.

I went to the search area with two members of my family. When I was told there were caves nearby I hoped that Joseph was alive. When I was told "A body has been found hanging from a tree and will need to be identified." I was in shock. I wanted to deny the reality of the situation.

My thoughts were racing, "*What do I do first? Who needs to be told? Where are the telephone numbers? How do I get there?*" I did some things on autopilot, such as telephoning family, answering questions, and making statements at the police station.

When I heard news that my husband had died, it shattered my life. Nothing from the past prepared me for the intensity of my feelings. In the past Joseph was always found or telephoned before he would go to hospital, there was always hope. Now the hope had gone.

Then there was the confusion as to why I was being questioned about his last hours leading up to his disappearance. I had been told that his body was to be identified. I was asked if I would do it the next morning. I agreed to do this, however when I got to the morgue someone else had been there just before me. I still insisted to go to say my goodbyes. We had been on a journey of this mental illness that affected us both. I needed to see Joseph, to say goodbye, to let him go!

During the period my husband was missing I had been told another person was also missing in the area. I knew my husband had a history of suicidal thoughts and at times acted upon those thoughts. It wasn't the first time he had made a noose. Although someone else identified the body, I had to see him for myself.

It was later that I realised the role of chaplain had a far-reaching effect on the people at the scene. The chaplain was there, and his presence helped me through one of the most difficult times in my life. There was no debriefing after a traumatic incident. The police gave me information about a counselling service.

After I had been to the morgue we started travelling home. On the way I received a telephone call from the police station asking what time I would be arriving. I was to call in on the way back to the city. When we arrived at the police station I found that there were three men who wanted to take the car and the belongings that were in the car. Joseph had been married before, thinking it was the right thing to do, I asked another person to organise the funeral. I did say that I wanted to have input into the service. With the proviso that it would be at the church we both attended.

During the time Joseph was missing. I was given a tape to listen to while driving. I was on my own. The words of a song kept going around in my head. The things that I thought of were interesting. So many people were affected. Reminiscing helped me get through. I would have preferred to forget as the words are often too painful to recall. Words and thoughts can bring the experience back as though the experiences happened yesterday. I wrote things down hoping to make sense of it all.

On arriving home, I opened the door to our home I noticed that items had been removed. I thought that *I am resilient. I grew up in the country*. Many personal items were taken along with memorabilia of ten years together. The shock of being told that someone had already been in the house. The garage had been broken into. My response to all this was not to go after anything that was taken. I saw it as being downsized real fast. The person who took these items obviously needed my things more than I did. Or so they may have thought. I was not going to fight over material things. Looking after my emotional and psychological health was far too important than to allow someone's behaviour affect my spirit. I wanted to keep my peace.

I found the lock on the garage had been changed, and there was an unexpected expense to get a locksmith to come to replace all the locks on the doors and windows. When I was finally able to get into the garage, I found that two dinner sets and cutlery sets were in the garage. It had been understood these items would be for my two children. It was evident that someone had a set of keys to be able to get in after Joseph's death was confirmed. It certainly answered any questions that I had as to why no one turned up at the search when they knew about it twelve hours before.

The following Sunday, it was raining heavily. I had decided to leave the washing on the clothesline while I attended church. My plan was to take them off when I returned home about two hours later. On returning from church I again discovered that someone had come to the house. I discovered all the washing had been taken off the clothesline. I couldn't find it anywhere.

Several days later, I had a call from the person who was organising the funeral. She gave me dates, time, told where the burial would take place. I was also told where his body was going to be buried. A car was organised to pick me up, take me to the service and onto the cemetery. All appeared to be going well until the end of the church service. What happened next I did not expect. The coffin was about to be taken out when the congregation was asked to remain seated while my two daughters and I were to walk behind the coffin. As we were waiting beside the car which had picked us up, the coffin had been placed in the hearse. No one appeared from the congregation for several minutes. A friend appeared, stood beside us before saying "I've just phoned work. I'm following you to make sure you are OK." It was then I heard that the congregation had just been told Joseph is not being buried where I was told. I stood in shock, thinking it can't get any worse when I heard someone say "Don't worry. We have the body." The coffin was in the hearse just in front of where we were standing. We all burst out laughing.

What could you do? When the congregation started coming outside looking as though they had no idea how I was going to react. It just added to the things being taken at the house. I knew all eyes would have been on me and how I would handle this new information. I needed to keep my peace.

With suicide, there is no more hope for a relationship with the other person. No one told me how much worse it could be when the person actually succeeds in taking their life. No words can describe the devastating emotional pain I experienced during this time.

During the last episode, which lasted around six weeks he refused to get help. I went to the medical professions, the mental health team, the police, the chamber of magistrate, the court. I tried everything I could do to get some help. All the signs were there to get help. Only a chamber of magistrate listened. He had experience with mental health issues, suggested going to court. No one else would listen.

On that last day when I saw Joseph alive, he made many telephone calls. He also made an appointment with a psychologist for us both to attend on the following Monday. He had been missing for six days before his body was found in a mountain.

The Psychologist who he had made an appointment with was there on the end of the telephone when the body was found. She came to the funeral, gave me her home telephone number; this was also a lifeline. I didn't telephone her at home, but knowing I could was powerful. The police were very good. They gave me information for grief counsellors. Surprise, surprise, after making phone calls to the numbers I was told there was no help. Thank goodness attitudes toward a person who lost a person by a traumatic death are changing. I discovered that sometimes I needed to walk alone to drop off any negative energy from people who didn't believe me when I did say anything about my loss.

My healing began when a Chaplain took me where the body was found. I had arranged with the Chaplain and with a person who had been on the search and knew the spot. My friend, Barbara and I walked together up this mountainside. It had recently been raining and the ground was damp. There appeared to be no trees with branches. We were shown a lone tree with a branch growing between some rocks that were placed like steps. Barbara speaking out loud said, "You have finally got me bushwalking." It reminded me of the time when Joseph was trying to get a walking group together to walk on trails through the mountain. I placed a ribbon and a bunch of flowers at the base of the tree.

CHAPTER 18
Aftermath of Suicide

It was eight weeks after the first Christmas and New Year without Joseph. I felt disconnected and decided to drive to another state to visit family. I packed my car, drove to the next state to be with my family.

After I had travelled seven hours I stopped for lunch. While sitting at the table in the restaurant I wrote this on a serviette. It has helped me many times since.

You came into this life as a gift from God
You left a gift to me from God
Just what I needed in the journey of life
Your love, care & concern for all who came into your path
You always wanted to know more
What you knew was never enough
You were striving to give your best
You left behind a legacy of memories
Things you taught, your attention to detail
Many loved you

The torment in your soul was too much to bear
You have gone to a better place
We are better for knowing you
Thank you for your life
What you gave me
Your life was not in vain
Your death has not been forgotten
Your life will make a difference to this world
Your passing will bring change to many
My world is a better place for having known you.

While I drove long distances, I sought God, "Why am I feeling this way?" My friends didn't visit. Family stayed away. No support groups to be found. If I kept going who would notice? I had been through a traumatic event where Joseph was missing for six days. There had been so many losses around this time. Within eight weeks after the funeral, no one had come to my home. It was then I realised "No one came to visit me at home."

Three months after Joseph died, I didn't have any visitors. I invited a friend for lunch. When I brought it up that I had not had anyone come to visit since the funeral.

She said "I didn't know what to do." She was a genuine person who cared about me. It was through this experience that my journey began with a vision; to change mindsets about the way that things have "always been done this way." The question that I am left with is why did she feel that she didn't know what to do? Is this the way most people think? They don't know what to do? I saw a need for a bridge between the family who is hurting in the church/ community. In a time of personal crisis we ask ourselves "Who will help me in this situation? From the carers they often wonder "What can we do to help?

My journey began by looking for a support group, but I didn't fit into any box where there was support. It appeared my situation was not in their criteria of assistance. The timing was wrong was another reason that I was given. It is too soon. Why it is too soon to be connected to other human beings? I rang places because I wanted to be connected. It took a lot of courage to do that.

I knew enough from training on grief issues, my life experience to know that a need I had was to be with people who would take time to listen. I wanted someone to just be with me in person to help me focus on the practical issues.

I had felt angry because it was his choice to die. He made that decision to leave before his time. No one ever told me about how painful grief could be. At times, I feel empty when I think of the loss. Yet I have felt angry because it was his choice to die. He made that decision to leave before his time. No one ever told me about how painful grief could be. At times I was frightened of the depth of my emotions, the sense of being on a roller coaster. It was at those times that I needed to know that another person was near. I withdrew at other times because I feared my reactions towards other people. I cried heaps. I'd wake up finding tears flowing freely and at other times, just cried uncontrollably. I became aware that I needed to let it happen, knowing that I would get through this.

The question, "What could I have done different" loomed. In the end I know that I did everything I could to help my husband with his illness. Accepting the reality of the loss is still hard at times. I realised that I needed to be able to look after myself emotionally, physically, and spiritually. In the early days, it was a good friend who kept in touch, showed care and concern, and helped immensely. Over time, I have fortunate to have had people around who have accepted that grieving is a process. This trust has been a precious gift; it has helped me in my journey. I realized that I only had so much emotional energy. I made some decisions that helped me get through. I prioritised my life giving myself permission to grieve. Although it is taking time to accept the reality of Joseph's death. I know that he is finally at peace.

I began to learn what Joseph did leading up to his death. Some things were a shock, but each part gave me answers. I'd thought we were debt free when he stopped taking his medication. After his death, I found letters, debts, which gave some answers. He used the credit card to the maximum, knowing that it would be paid out on his death. He borrowed money which had insurance, where he couldn't have it paid out if he took his life under fourteen days. I found a long tape and played it over many times until I no longer could put myself through that. I put the tape aside after I had it typed out to read at a later date.

A tape for the family was in the garage. Both were taped about three weeks before his funeral.

Although I couldn't organise a meal, I ordered home deliveries for about six weeks until I got back on track. Frozen dinners helped me get through. Going to the supermarket was difficult emotionally. Going back to anywhere we had visited was traumatic but one thing at a time I am revisiting places making new memories.

The year after Joseph's death, I completed an advanced diploma in pastoral ministry. This year had been put aside to write a thesis on 'Bridging the Gap' between Families in Crisis within the Church and Community. This came out of a friend who told me that she didn't know what to do.

As I looked back over the first year since Joseph's death, I realised that this experience was a significant part of my life. I came to accept that he is no longer alive. A revelation I got was that I had known Joseph for twelve years. I had over fifty years of travelling along my road of living. The years we were together were a significant part of my journey. I have accepted that he is no longer alive, he will not return. I know that the process of healing will take time. I have allowed the healing to happen by experiencing the loss. I have found a place for the memories of Joseph that will give honour to our life together. I have continually adjusted to my life without my husband. This adjusting is allowing me to be able to go on from one destination to another. I know that I will again be able to take the time to invest in the future.

After my husband died, I spent the first year contacting places for some sort of support. There were groups for parents who had lost a child. I contacted one group but couldn't interrupt the group by attending at that time. I went on a search. I read a lot of books on grief. I came across an article on 'Companions of Grief Support' in the local paper. This was a one-day workshop at a Community Health Centre for people who had lost a person by suicide. I attended this weekend nine months after Joseph's death. Two months later I went to a weekend event which was a safe and caring environment. It gave me an opportunity to move through the grief I had from the loss.

I wanted to learn more, to be involved in helping others who were grieving the loss of a loved one. During the second year, I attended a support group for a number of weeks. Each session was self-contained, so it allowed people to go in and out of the program.

A workshop, weekend and a weekly program were all part of my process of healing. My story could not be told without acknowledging the different support groups that helped me along the way.

During the second year after my husband died, I had an opportunity to go back to England to see his family, visiting places that we had been to together. Joseph was born in the United Kingdom and he had taken me back to England twice during our marriage. I realised when I was in Scotland that I was fulfilling the dream of places we had talked about seeing together. It was during this time I realised that I was finalising all the dreams that we had together, making new memories for myself.

While travelling overseas I visited a Cathedral in Cheshire, England. As I walked into the entrance I saw a bookshop right in the entrance where there was a stand with cards on it. The first card I picked up had the following written on it. It was written by
Helen Keller

"When one door of happiness closes;
Another opens;
But often we look so long at the closed door
That we do not see the one that has been open for us".
-Helen Keller

This year had given me time to reflect and get new dreams as a single unit. It has been a year of pushing through; going to places we had been to. I saw it as an opportunity to saying good-bye to the memories of the past -and to dream again.

Nine years after, I had got a new life and felt safe again. The years in between have been learning to be kind to myself and having people in my life who have given me a safe haven to live and rebuild.

CHAPTER 19
Being Kind to Myself

On reflection, I became skilled at being kind to myself. I wrote a list of things that I did to help me along my journey. When it was necessary, I would revisit my list to see what I could do to help myself.

First, I kept going to church. It gave me a day to focus on being with people

I kept a book on the table to write down ideas and things I wanted to do. When I thought of something, I wrote it down. Some of the list included names of friends or family and place I wanted to visit.

I kept a journal and wrote down my thoughts and feelings. At times after I read the entry I would destroy the pieces of paper.

I would use a diary to schedule the things I needed to do. It was so easy to do things randomly, but I soon realised that I needed to have routine in my life. This included going to bed each night. I planned to be in bed by 10.00p.p. I also included times for meals and snacks.

Having a pet helped. I had a dog and took it for morning walks.

I found I had more bubble baths during the tough times.

I telephoned someone at certain times each week.

I allowed myself time to think and reflect.

I found a support group with people going through a similar situation. Listening to others talk would often give me an answer in all my confusion. Spending time with people who have been in the same or similar situation before me gave me hope. I would find out as much information as I could to help myself. I picked up pamphlets everywhere I went, just in case I had a need for the information later.

Support groups would give me a network, a place to allow myself to open up, to find acceptance. I was able to make a decision not to isolate myself as a result of someone else's choice. It was the beginning of healing of past hurts.

I attended two groups where I experienced a weekend where I could spend time for myself with others who had experienced a loss. It was an opportunity to participate, to interact with other families without shame or judgement.

When it was necessary, I was open to see a counsellor. I made a choice to not do it on my own. I wanted to be with like-minded people who didn't judge me but were willing to challenge me in my thinking. I made every morning a new day, that it was the first day of the rest of my life. Lessons I discovered was that choices that I made could affect my life in a way that could be life changing. It was a defining moment.

CHAPTER 20

Impact of Suicide

Historically, my first experience was a suicide in progress was before my husband, Joseph first attempted suicide. Six and a half years later his death was by suicide. I have asked myself what I have discovered during this season in my life. Is there is anything I can share that may help others?

I continually get shown the impact suicide has on people of all ages. The older members of families can be left out of the loop of information sharing of their grief can be overlooked.

Bereavement holds many facets. Looking back, each experience had its own difficulties. While I was dealing with my own grief, there was a closing of the ranks by friends and family. No one talked about the subject. There were so many people left with unanswered questions.

During this period, it was like walking on eggshells. I found the wife was not part of the treatment plan. This is an area where I saw that confidentiality went too far. As a wife, I wasn't listened to, but as a welfare worker, I had no problems getting assistance to get another person help. I was the same person but as a wife I discovered what I saw what was happening to a loved one was disregarded. Homicide / suicide were very real. I believe my earlier training was the reason I am alive today.

My healing began after my husband died by suicide. Joseph had been missing six days before he was found in the mountains. The morning before my husband went missing he made an appointment with a Psychologist for both of us to meet on the following Monday. Keeping the appointment time I telephoned the psychologist to let her know that I could not attend as I was with the police discussing a missing person. It was like Joseph had put in place someone for me to talk with.

At the search site, there were the police, other support people, and a Chaplain. I recall thinking this will affect the people here who are part of this search. The people who were part of the search have families to go home to.

The chaplain without judgement stayed with me. He was there when Joseph's body was found. I recall being handed a business card while saying to me "When you are ready I will take you to the site." The police gave me information to talk to a grief counsellor, but sadly they didn't work with a person left behind by suicide. It was suggested that to speak to someone, I would need to wait at least ten months to get over the angry stage. This was not helpful at all but shown how little was known about bereavement after suicide.

I was able to speak with the psychologist that my husband had made an appointment with after I had been told a body was found. The psychologist also came to the funeral to support me. I was given her home telephone number. I recall going to see her couple of times, but the lack of funds stopped me from continuing as I began to think about having a good friend would be just as helpful. I had one good friend; we met at a coffee shop many times of the day or evening. One evening after closing time, we were still talking. The manager came over saying you can stay here while we clean up. We will let you know when we are ready to leave.

Surprisingly, after Joseph's death, I didn't even get a casserole or cake brought to my home. This was not a normal death. However, three months after my husband's death I invited a friend for lunch I told her she was the first person to come to my home. She said "I didn't know what to do." This was the catalyst of writing a thesis 'Bridging the Gap" It was a bridge between the families in crisis within the Church Community. Later I spoke about the aftermath of suicide at a suicide prevention conference.

I quickly discovered there are some life events that are just not talked about. Living with a person who considers suicide is a difficult topic to speak about, can be the hidden secret. Regarding my husband's mental illness; it felt like the unspoken truth that went on within the family, friends and work colleagues. There was the pressure not to mention how the person died. I was told not to talk to this person or that person. Others were told to stay away from me. Surprisingly, many years later a person who was part of a group I had attended regularly said "We didn't believe you." Those words say it all.

Writing has been cathartic in my journey of personal growth and healing. The grief was different to any other grief I had experienced. The sense of isolation and loneliness was insurmountable. The impact of the word *suicide* had affected any social life as I had known it. Suddenly there were no invitations but hope came after attending a weekend workshop and a weekly program. This began a journey of hope, a search of meaning.

Life went on no matter the hopes of the future had gone. No matter how much I tried to keep going, the pain was still being raw at anniversaries. The loss of family, friends, lack of trust, and the non-belief of what is happening for the person left behind weighed heavily.

Looking back it was the contact with the chaplain at the scene, the follow-up with a psychologist that was the catalyst toward healing and hope for the future.

A workshop over two days with two facilitators who were also survivors was powerful in moving forward ten months after my loss. A weekend workshop, a weekly program were all part of my process of my healing. I found common experience within a group environment where I could be vulnerable with talking about loss and grief has been beneficial to my recovery of loss. To have someone to trust with my feelings, emotions, hopes, and dreams for me was essential to my recovery from the loss.

My lived experience here taught me many things. Bringing everything out into the open has given me an inner strength that continues to grow. Sharing my story opens the door for others to know that they are not alone.

There is one thing I need to share. My husband's workplace that has been a constant. They have a retirees association; each year since just before Christmas I have received a Christmas cake. This cake has been a constant that Joseph has been acknowledging Joseph has been remembered. How nice is that?

Joseph, your life was not in vain; your death has not been forgotten. I believe it was this experience that allowed my healing for the memory to be unlocked so I could have total healing of the past.

I grew up in the country and was grounded in knowing that God loved me. Life has had many twists and turns since. I have been able to keep my faith knowing that I haven't been alone.

It was while being trained to be a volunteer telephone counsellor I had a first-hand experience of a friend who called after taking an overdose of pills. I heard later that it had been a suicide in progress.

Nothing prepared me for the experience of a person who makes a suicide attempt or the finality of suicide within my family. Through life experience I have seen the evidence in my life that God has gone before me. .*Denial* is a very strong word. When we married, my husband was travelling well with no indication there was a problem.

We would have been married ten years the day after the funeral. He died overlooking where we had our honeymoon ten years before. When I went to the site, it was such a peaceful place. Knowing Joseph, I could understand why that was his final resting place.

A day that is imprinted on my mind forever began on a beautiful sunny day. It was Easter Monday 1993. We were going to have lunch with friends. My husband took my car out of the garage; said "You go. I'll stay home to get some work done." As I was driving away I felt a sense of doom. The only indication there was a problem was the way my husband spoke. The voice was soft but there was something about it that gave me alarms bells. We always did things together. It was out of character for him not to come with me.

This incident was before we had mobile telephones. When I got to our friends' place, I asked to use their telephone to contact a member of the family to ask if he could go to see Joseph while I was out. Two members of his family went to our home.

What they found was a suicide in progress. It wasn't what I expected to hear. This was my first personal experience of a suicide attempt by a loved one, and I was devastated. The difficult part was that Joseph had told his family that I was not to go to the hospital. They said, "He doesn't want to see you". This became the catch cry each time there was an attempt on his life. In the end, it was just the two of us trying to live life safely.

I quickly understood that there are some events that are just not talked about. These examples and other life experiences can the secret within a family. Living with a person who considers suicide is a difficult subject to speak about. This can be the hidden secret as each person sees something different.

I waited until the next morning to the hospital. I took a toiletry bag to see if I could at least leave that. At the hospital I was told he couldn't stay there, I would have to take him home. Here was a person, who the day before, had attempted suicide. He had told his family, "I don't want to see my wife." The car still had the hose attached in the garage. His family did not remove the hose for me.

The hospital was saying that I was to take him home. I was trying to get my head around all of this. I was being asked to take him home after an attempted suicide to a house where the car was still set up in the garage.

I believe my husband knew enough from his training in suicide prevention that he had to get help. He refused to leave the hospital before we were able to get him into a psychiatric hospital. There was no offer from the family or friends while quite traumatised by this I had to drive him. Not a wise move. . Where is the help for a family in crisis? I had to go home to remove the hose from the car myself.

I was in shock. At the hospital, there was no support for the family. I was not told anything at the hospital; it was confidential. I was his wife but no information was given to me. I wasn't told of his medications or how to help with the health problem. When I approached the hospital to speak to someone, I was told, "We thought you were doing OK." They appeared shocked that I wanted to talk to someone. I was told that I wasn't the patient.

After each episode, it was just the two of us trying to live life to make sense of it all. I discovered quickly there are some events are just not talked about. These examples, along with other life experiences, can be swept under the carpet. The best thing to possibly do is to hide the problem and forget about it as every member of the family and friends are all seeing something different.

We may live our lives doing all the right things; but, when things happen to someone we care about, it is the consequences of what they did that wc are left with, to work through and to try and make some sense of it.

It appeared the mental health system did not know a thing about suicide prevention or supporting the family. I was going through a dark tunnel and it was a lonely experience. Fortunately, with my work I had been instrumental in getting an Employee Assistance Program up and running and I had contact with the service. I went as often as was needed, usually every week for many months. Over the years, I was open to getting help for myself.

My husband was in hospital for three weeks and came home quite unwell. It was interesting how our lives changed. Suddenly there were no visitors during his hospital stay. Family and friends stayed away. I felt I was being judged when I was questioned and challenged that must have been a fight. There appeared to be no understanding that the person made the attempt to take his life was unwell. This episode began via a fear of retrenchment.

My journey with a person who considered suicide went on for six and a half years. I supported my husband throughout this time. When he well he was the man I married. When it changed I dealt with Joseph as a person with an illness.

I knew if I didn't have the strength to support and find out as much as I could, my husband wouldn't be alive as long as he was. He was a son, a father, and a grandfather. I did what I could to get Joseph to see his family, even when he wanted to withdraw from family and friends.

Looking back, I can pinpoint the day he had already made a decision to end his life this final time. Three weeks before, he had made tapes. He also had an insurance to cover the debts as long as he lived fourteen days; it covered death by suicide.

Typically, his attitude and behaviour was so out of character that it was a shock to watch a man who had such a high moral character change during these episodes. During his last episode, it was as if no one was going to change his mind. He resented me trying to get him help and he turned against me. Life was not easy. He told me to act as if I didn't live in the home so he could bring other women into the home.

He began to give possessions away, both his and mine. One day I came home and found that he had divided up the house, the blinds were torn down and there were no curtains hanging. He would at times get violent toward me and it became necessary to keep myself safe. I was in shock, not knowing what the next step would be. No one would hear my cry. I went to many people for help. His previous medical history did not appear to mean anything.

One day after I spoke to the psychiatrist, I was told to take someone with me when I went home. When I arrived, his car was there. As I walked into the house, there was my husband with a lady. Interestingly, his persona and how he even looked changed depending on where he was in the cycle of his mental health. I did not go back to the home for my safety. I could only let it take its course. The person I had with me said "He is convincing."

I later heard that he had met the lady with a big bunch of flowers and had put them in her car just before I arrived home. He had picked up a lady at McDonalds and she had been invited to our home.

- I went to the police for help.
- I went to the Chamber of Magistrate.
- I went to the mental health system.

With this background, it was a nightmare during the months leading up to the time my husband was missing and afterwards from people who did not want to accept that he had an illness. This road we travelled in most part alone from the time he was diagnosed with a Reactive Depression on Easter Monday in 1933. He was later diagnosed with Bipolar Disorder three years later. I felt so alone going through the trauma leading up to my husband's death.

I watched as my husband's mental health change, the episodes getting more dangerous. I have woken up with a rope tied to a tree out the front of the house. His family have been there and thought it was funny and played Tarzan on it. They went home and left it there.

There is another aspect I need to speak about. One Christmas Eve as we were travelling up the coast an episode happened that showed me how easy it would be for people to think it was a road accident when it would have been murder-suicide. Luckily, a way out came, and I was able to get help. The police put me in a refuge and said it was just a domestic and allowed him to go back home, and destroy my things and told his family I had left him.

It confirmed to me I couldn't get help within the family circle and even the psychiatrist wasn't helpful when I was concerned. It meant again it wasn't safe for me at home. There were the times I lived out of my car to keep myself safe. I couldn't go to my own children as I couldn't trust he wouldn't do something to them.

My fears were supported as during one of his many episodes he put an advertisement in the paper to meet a friend. It was a dangerous time for me. His children met this lady, but one night he put a noose up in the bedroom in our home. Joseph then took a knife and a petrol bomb to her house. Joseph told me later that he only stopped when he saw the blood where he had cut her. He called the police. I was contacted by a member of the family when Joseph was in a prison awaiting a court case. I was told that I would know what to do. I visited him while he had stays in two prisons while waiting to go to court for a bail hearing. Again I felt used by people who were pointing the finger at me for the trouble he was in by their actions and asking me to put up the bail. Feeling under pressure from family, who were present at the court I put up ten thousand dollars for bail, and Joseph was able to be in my care to go to the hospital. This meant that I was to drive him to the hospital an hour's drive away. This time it was for six weeks and during that time he was assessed before the next court date.

The psychiatrist said "I didn't expect this to happen". All I could say was "It didn't surprise me." I saw signs but I couldn't get anyone to listen. Instead of spending time in prison, Joseph had to do community service. Generally, after episodes Joseph would tell me about the lead up and how he thought and what he had planned to do.

There were many things that were done, including changing the gas outlet to come into the bedroom and a manhole in the floor. He placed a mat over the opening.

There was a time he wanted to learn to dance. We had visitors staying with us, and told them he wanted to learn to surprise me. He would have dinner at home and was always home by 9.00 p.m. To say the least when Joseph began to tell us that he "I had dinner at an Indian restaurant last night with my fiancée." I was in shock and didn't say anything at that time. But it did explain that the day before, I came home from work and he had moved some of his things into the spare bedroom. When I came home from work I saw two cups on the sink. I later discovered that he had bought an engagement, wedding ring, and eternity ring for her to prove she was the one. He had taken her to our home to show her that we were separated. That certainly explained why he had moved clothing into the spare room a few days before. No wonder his first family were confused. They only knew what he had chosen to tell them.

He had cashed in his superannuation. The crash came after all the money was spent. During this episode, I spoke to his psychiatrist about things are not adding up he told me that he was counselling him to leave the marriage. I was not involved in any part of his medical condition or support. As a wife, I was there to pick up the pieces.

When Joseph had started a relationship with another woman before his final attempt, he said to me before he went missing "I think I have done enough to make her hate me." It hit me that this is what Joseph did over the years. The other women were to get me to hate him, and then he'd feel remorse, wanting me to get him help. He spent lots of money on the other women. I guess who wouldn't like the red roses sent to their workplace? As things began to unfold about what my husband did leading up to his death, some things were a shock, but each part gave me answers.

I found a long tape. I played it over and over until I no longer could put myself through that, and I put it aside after I had it typed out to read at a later date. A tape for the family was in the garage. Both were taped about three weeks before his funeral. I no longer have these. Keeping them was holding me back emotionally and I was ready to move on.

I also gathered information after Joseph's death, the lady who he hurt was awarded victim compensation. I found that amazing as she knew of his illness. She answered an advertisement he put in the paper during a manic episode. Her employer was an advocate for suicide prevention; but out of desperation, when I spoke to him he supported their friendship. I just had to ride the storm. My husband comes to know about the inside of a prison and the woman was awarded money for her part in this journey.

Suicide is final; there is no more hope of a life with the other person. I have felt shock, hurt, confusion, loneliness and rejection. No one told me how much worse it could be when the person actually succeeds in taking his or her life. No words can describe the devastating pain and emotions I experienced after my husband's death by suicide.

We all have a story, we all have chapters in our lives, we have all had lessons in life that we have learnt something from. I have had many lessons and have tried to learn more about each situation and to make a difference. Some life experiences appear to be worse than others, but it is what we can do about our responses to our journey of life that we can use to make a difference.

Fifteen years after my interest began in suicide prevention began I wrote a book which was later published. There are many chapters and include lessons I gained knowledge from along the way. Families and friends are devastated, and getting the communication happening while there is so much pain and blame may never happen.

Life has to go on and we come to terms with life and making a difference within the community. The best thing I learnt was to gain knowledge. It helped me with taking the fear out of the situation.

Get a good network about you. You may never need it, but if do, it is more precious than gold. Having good friends to support each other and look after ourselves in the process. I had one friend who was my coffee friend. I could telephone her and she would just say I will meet you.

Today I have got a new life. I feel safe again. I have taken time to look at different aspects of the journey with a person who was suicidal. Today I live life, and when things from the past come up, I know I can say it doesn't matter it is in the past. It is energy draining to keep it inside. I need to talk to someone and make sense of it all. The energy comes back with new insight.

The hardest thing to accept is the fact that I was a target for homicide. Even being apart didn't stop the manhole being put in the floor before he left, and coming in to turn the gas around in the bedroom.

I have recalled all the times I had the gas heater on in the bedroom and not had a problem. Then the night while on my own, turned the gas heater on and coughed all night. Finally, I telephoned the ambulance. At the hospital, I was told my oxygen level was low. It was suggested that it was from the coughing. It took time to put things in perspective. Before the house was rented out, he said "Get the gas people to check the gas in the bedroom". A worker was blamed for putting it in wrong but I now have put it all together and accepted who did it.

I already knew if he was in hospital, he could still leave and come home. Home for me was not a safe place during these times. So I really wasn't surprised when he showed me the manhole in the lounge room floor. He said it was in case I changed the locks.

If my story can help just one person, it will be worthwhile. Be open to their story and don't doubt. I knew when I was wasting my time telling anyone. It takes too much energy to be counselled. Just listen and be there for the person who is sharing their story. I would in the end, know how to keep myself safe. I needed someone who would walk with me for a time. Just being there sometimes just listening would be invaluable. Yes, sometimes it would be a safe bed for the night just to get some rest.

Listen to the stories, and you will see the way each person in the family is being told what they want to hear. Blaming a partner always is an easy target. I heard it constantly. The years in between have been learning to be kind to myself and having people in my life who have given me a safe haven to live, rebuild.

I had the opportunity to go to Melbourne for the second 'Post Vention Conference' and a workshop 'Living Hope Suicide Bereavement Training Program'. At this conference a memory quilt was unveiled.

One of the moments that meant a lot to me was having my husband's photo on a memory quilt. In all there were sixty four photos on the quilt.

Beside Joseph's photo I had the words written beside it.

"Your life was not in vain
Your death has not been forgotten."

If my experience can help give one person, this will be all worthwhile.

Where to from here? There are new dreams for the future. The unveiling of the quilt meant that my husband's life is recognised finally after nearly ten years. It was one of those healing moments. I wanted to shout to the world. "This was my husband". We had a great life together when he was well. He had an illness, and we had to deal with life with the mental health system which had in my experience no understanding of suicide prevention. Training should be part of all people who work in care giving roles in the community.

He did live. When I saw his photo, Joseph on the Memory Quilt I was relieved that finally the world can see him as a human being. I want the world to see that he was a good person; he was a husband, father, grandfather, and friend. The people he loved should not feel the shame of what he did and how he died.

The word *suicide* and the feeling of shame divide family and all who knew him. Not only do you lose a loved one but you can lose every person who knew the deceased so the significant other can be so alone in the journey of dealing with the trauma and ongoing grief. There are so many unspoken words.

I met a person who told me her son had died by suicide and she had not told anyone in the family he had died until four months later. There is so much shame and lack of acknowledgement of the way the person died. It is like it all has to be hidden. Let's continue to bring it out of the closet.

There needs to be a system where the family are brought together as soon as practicable with a person trained in this area. Each person has a part of the puzzle, and together they may make a completed painting.

My hope for the future is that suicide is treated the same as any disaster. The initial response is to get all the people involved in the lead up to suicide; first responders, family and friends to be debriefed. The pieces of the puzzle that can make a picture can begin the healing process. I have no doubt that each person had been told different things. Dealing with the trauma is just as important as dealing with the grief of the loss.

It was after a conversation with a friend whose grandchild had attempted suicide and another grandparent who told me her grandson had died by suicide that I realized the impact that this has on each person in the family as well as friends and colleagues. Memories came flooding back about the unspoken truth about the things that have happened that went on within the family, friends, and work colleagues. There was the pressure not to mention how the person died. The flashbacks were as though it had just happened. Surviving the impact of how my husband died has given me hope by looking at my own spirituality, hope, meaning, and direction. My healing began after my husband died by suicide.

I have found writing has been cathartic in my journey of personal growth and healing. The bereavement was different to any other grief I had experienced. The sense of isolation and loneliness was insurmountable.

I have found the impact of the word *suicide* had affected any social life as I had known it. Suddenly there were no invitations but hope came after attending a weekend workshop and a weekly program.

Life went on but the hopes of the future had gone no matter how much I tried to keep going the pain can still be raw at anniversaries. The loss of family, friends, lack of trust, and the non-belief of what is happening for the person left behind weighed heavily. Looking back it was contact with the Chaplain at the scene and the follow up with a Psychologist that was the catalyst toward healing and hope for the future. While I began searching for spirituality I found common experience within a group environment where I could be vulnerable with talking about loss and grief.

CHAPTER 21

Time to Heal the Loss of Innocence

It was time for me to deal with the loss of innocence and to report a crime fifty four years later. I realised that memories don't fade as the years grow dim. It was like yesterday; sometimes I was in the moment. Children had no voice, but as an adult, I do. A significant event has been a catalyst in making this report of a crime committed against me when I was nine years old.

Over the years, events were happening that would trigger the past. Each time it was as much as I could cope with at the time. I was attending a reunion going into the area where I grew up. I wanted to run from the area. I started to be aware of having some fear. When I would visit with family, I could feel safe to cope for a short time. At times I would leave abruptly, after leaving myself a way out if I was feeling uncomfortable.

I recall always feeling safe while I was at church and school, but not at home, starting when I was nine years of age. At the reunion, I met up with an old school friend.

We were best friends and she would come and stay at our house. I recall needing her to stay and sleepover. When I was ten years of age she suddenly left the area and went to live in the city. On meeting, we hugged each other, and I got quite upset and said to her "You were my friend, and you disappeared." I asked her what happened, why she had left. She told me she'd left after her baby sister had died. She was very upset and her grandmother took her to live with her.

I started to have dreams about the nightmares I had as a child. I was dreaming that I was screaming out that I was alive in a coffin and no one was hearing my silent screams "I'm here, I'm in here."

Memories came back of leaving home to work at the age of sixteen and a half because I no longer felt safe in the community. Leaving home and starting work gave a place to sleep and nurses lived in nurses' quarters during those years. At nineteen, I left the district altogether. A year later, I came home for a month but left the area very quickly after on one particular night. I was sleeping I was woken up by a person going around the house and knocking. When I asked who was there the man said "You know who it is."

The voice I heard was enough, and I thought "*He is back, but won't leave me alone.*" I had been working at the railway gates while my parents were away on holidays. Fortunately they came home a day early and after my father called out, the man left.

Leading up to this incident, I had spoken to his brother earlier that day. He had stopped at the railway gates while waiting for a train to pass. This innocent conversation has shown me how saying anything could have a consequence as I didn't realise that speaking about what I was doing would mean the information was shared with someone who had in the past caused me grief.

After my parents came home, I left the next day.

Since the reunion, I have travelled to the area to the area more regularly as my elderly mother was in high care in a hostel in a regional town. I began meeting people who kept bringing up the man's name whom I'll call Jack. My mother mentioned that Jack had been out to visit her. I froze and asked myself, *"Why would Jack visit my mother after what he did to her daughter."* During one visit to the area, while driving my mother from one place to another, my mother said "that is where Jack lives." Another person showed a photo album and said "That is Jack. You remember him."

At each encounter, I froze and could not say I could recall his name or respond to the conversation. This person's name was being put in front of me and I felt powerless about doing anything or saying anything. I felt the fear of a nine-year old child who should have felt safe in her own bed and a fifteen year old girl who should have been able to walk safely on a country road at night going home from fellowship.

I finally opened up to the friend who knew me during the first incident, and told her what had happened to me. I told her every person has mentioned his name. She asked if she had. I said "Yes." It took some visits before I finally let her know who he was.

I began having nightmares and telephoned a crisis line. During the conversation, the person at the other end of the line said I need to say his name. I mentioned his name, and the emotional dam burst. I knew I had to follow through with this and take my life back; I had to take my personal power back.

After having dreams about the nightmares I had as a child. I began having dreams of confronting Jack. I realised I was not emotionally strong enough and did not have a support group around me to help me through. It was during this time I decided to seek out a support group.

The incident was a crime to me, and I needed to have this acknowledged: it had happened, and the perpetrator had to take responsibility for taking away someone's innocence. I don't want it to happen to another person. I have no way of knowing if he is a safe person to be around.

My greatest fear was that this person would be at my mother's funeral. I want to be able to go to the funeral and not having the fear of running into him. An incident happened that enhanced this concern. I took my mother to a medical appointment. As we were sitting talking to people around us, I sensed a person had come in the door and was standing in front of the reception desk.

Suddenly, in the middle of a conversation, I felt as though I was being crushed, and e a black cloud came over me. I thought I was going to die. Fear had struck my chest, and I could hardly breathe and the pain was unbearable. I quietly continued sitting and trying to get my breath.

My mother kept saying that it was so and so, "You know Jack." My mother was unaware of the body memories I was having. A person was sitting on either side of me but there was a spare seat next to the lady beside me. As this person walked in the door I suddenly felt like I was back in that coffin. It was only the week before I had told a girlfriend about what Jack had done to me.

My mother spoke to Jack and called him by name. As soon as I heard the voice, I thought my heart was going to come out of my chest. I was feeling terror. He sat two seats from me. There were four seats in a row. I was sitting between my mother and another person.

My mother and Jack talked across me. I felt rude but I felt I was in survival mode. I remembered that I had my mobile telephone out. It had been the week before that I had told a friend who I went to school with what I had happened to me as a child- the first time I had verbally told my story. To stop myself from shaking, I texted my friend and wrote "The rapist is here".

With my heart pounding, I was unable to speak. When the lady who had been sitting next to me went in to see the doctor my mother and Jack continued to talk. They spoke about how safe it was growing up in our area. They talked about how they could leave windows and doors open and know everything was safe.

Mum finally mentioned, "This is Joan".

Jack said "I thought it was Joan;" and when he asked me "Where do you live now?"

I was terrified and felt the powerlessness I had as a child and a young girl. I refused to answer. I felt that I was being rude in front of my mother, but as I had never told her she would not have understood my behaviour.

My mother continued saying how nice this person had been over the years. My mother kept talking over me to him. I refused to get into the conversation. Finally, a breakthrough came when I received a telephone call from my sister. "Thank you, Lord." I had a way out. I turned to my mother and said that I need to answer this telephone call, and went outside. I know that whatever situation I have been in, God is one step ahead. He is preparing my journey, and He will lead me through it. When I finished the telephone call from my sister I looked up, and a family member appeared nearby. After I said that Mum was inside waiting to see the doctor the person went in to see her and stayed until she was finished and walked out to the car with her.

This friendliness with my mother who I had not told what he had done to me during her lifetime brought me to believe he would be bold enough to attend her funeral. As it happened, he died just after I reported the crime to the police.

That day at the doctor's office, the first thing I wanted to do was to run to the police station a few doors away from where I was. But practicality took over, and I knew that I had to get my mother back to the nursing home. I still couldn't tell my mother after all these years. She went to her grave not knowing what had happened to her daughter.

I had not seen this person who was the perpetrator for a long time before that day. Once his presence came into the area where I was had shown me the trauma and the knowing within of the effect that this person did to me when I was a little girl was still within my spirit and the story was to be told.

It took fifty four years to report the incident. I awoke one morning at 4.00a.m. and knew that was the day that I would take the statement that I had written to the police. I travelled back to the police station where the incident had taken place. It was the toughest day, with the fear surfacing. I wanted it all to go away, but I also had a knowing I had to tell someone my story. It was a way of acknowledging what had happened and hoping it would be a healing of the past.

What did I learn that day I reported the incident to the police?

- It was a crime.
- I didn't do anything wrong.
- It wasn't my fault.

I also learnt that just reporting the crime can be all a person may need to do and it gets closure. The next stage was to get the police to bring the person in and question them. There could be a meeting at the police station with the perpetrator. I heard even after this time that charges could be laid.

After I had reported the crime to the police I found myself speaking to a lady whom I knew was a sister-in law of the person who had sexually abused me as a child. She kept asking if I remember Jack as he was in Sydney with lung cancer.

When I heard that the perpetrator had died, there was a sense of relief. He could no longer hurt me or anyone else. I won't run into him again and be confronted by him. He probably had no idea how his action changed one person's life so dramatically. There is consequence to everything we do in life and everything we don't do that we should do. Life goes on regardless.

CHAPTER 22

Looking to the Future

These incidents may have begun over fifty years ago however seeing this person brought the feelings back of fear and terror that I had so long ago. It was a significant event that changed my life forever, taking my innocence and losing the sense of feeling safe in my childhood and beyond. As the memories were coming back one piece at a time I found a support group.

I WANTED TO TAKE CONTROL OF MY LIFE.

I WANTED THE SENSE OF EMPOWERMENT.

I WANTED TO FEEL SAFE.

I was travelling with a friend who wanted to travel through the village where we grew up. There was a club there, and he was talking about going to see if there was anyone we knew there. We met people who remembered me. I recall was meeting a neighbour from my childhood. I had a sense of being safe and the stirring of memories of my younger years. I began recalling friends who had visited after I had left home. I began to think there were good times, and an underlying traumatic event shattered that sense of feeling safe.

Life is full of changes and as I was reminded that our path had crossed at an earlier reunion. It was at that reunion that I met the perpetrator who was talking with a group of people, and everything was a blank after that. I did not go to any other gatherings during that week end. I recalled getting away from there quickly and driving over the gutter, drove over the gutter damaging the muffler of the car. I had my children in the car and had to get the car fixed in the local town before driving back to the city.

At the time, I did not realise the significance of that incident and what had happened to affect me in such a way.

Life experiences can be painful at times, but we can't hide forever; it comes out in the end and needs to be dealt with.

When I began to write my story, suddenly everywhere I went, the perpetrator's name kept coming up. He also visited my mother, and my mother told me how she always liked him.

After the death of my husband I had been questioned by the police. It was part of their learning more about what happened. After having to answer questions on the day my husband's body was found, I started to think more about going to the police about what happened when I was a child. As I recalled that questioning, I decided that it was time to put it down on paper. It was very cathartic to go through that period, which was often painful and with many tears. After I had finished the report, I had put it in the boot of the car for a time when I was ready to go to the police station to report it.

The day that made it very clear that I was ready started off with a four hour drive to pick up my mother from a nursing home to go to an appointment. I recall it was a beautiful day. The sun was shining and my mother was so happy to get out of the nursing home to go for a drive. Nothing prepared me to for what was to happen when we were sitting in the waiting room. The waiting room was packed with people waiting for their turn to see the specialist, but before that, other staff would take each patient in for their part of the examination before actually seeing the specialist. With people coming and going, there was a lot of movement, and activity. As we were waiting our turn, we chatted with the people near us.

What I did learn that day was being in the area where a person who had violated my body as a young child could be just as strong without even seeing or knowing that the person was there. It still affected my soul.

A personal journey of life has been like there is a destination to be reached. The destination for me had many pathways before reaching that destination. From feeling safe at home to a traumatic event happening as a nine year old and how that event has been an influence in my life. A chain of events happened to get to the destination of finally being able to lay the trauma to rest and find peace in my soul.

What I come to know is that life is like a series of journeys. Along the road there are choices to be made. Sometimes I travelled alone, sometimes someone walked with me, and at other times I stopped awhile in one place, and went to a group of people who had travelled the way before me.

Like any adventure, I have stayed awhile in one place, and then division would happen- perhaps a holiday or a decision to take a trip. The journey has been like having a roadmap many roads, lanes, streets, suburbs, towns, and cities. Although I have had the destination in mind and have done all the preparation to get to the destination at the appointed time, there can also be obstacles. The trip may not go according to plan. I learnt not to focus on the circumstances.

How I managed depended on my reaction to the crisis. Many things can happen on the journey, such as roadwork to hold us up, or takes a detour that take us many miles out of our way and to places I didn't expect. The journey takes on a different perspective and unexpected turns.

Change of direction can be caused by too much happening at once. There were some things that have helped along the way, including writing down the things that has helped so I could go back and reflect on how far I have come.

No experience in my life has been wasted. Each trial has shown me so much about myself and has launched me to do something about the lessons that I have learnt. The journey to a better life made me a stronger, happier person.

God turns negatives into positives. Suffering took me to a level of understanding I would never have reached without the journey. Every stage of life presented a lesson to be learnt. In everything, I give thanks and use what was in my hands.

On reflection, life has been full of challenges. There has been a new beginning after every challenge. Not all the situations have been my choosing. But there is a consequence of what a person does, and as it was said in

Alcoholics Anonymous, with one alcoholic in the family no fewer than five people are affected. It is what we do with the pain that comes with those challenges.

I do believe God is healing us and he wants us whole as He intended us to be.

I spent some time back in the area where my journey began. I believe God had me there for a season. Through memories I believe that I was being shown in my spirit an area to work on from the past. The spirit was telling me to report it, but it so long ago and in the "too hard" basket. The person's name was mentioned in many conversations, either in the area I grew up in or when I went to the other side of the country. Since I reported the incidents, his name has only been mentioned once while I visited a market day. She kept asking if I remember Jack and that he was in the city and had lung cancer. While this conversation was taking place a couple came along and interrupted the and once again there was a sense again that God had put people in my path to help me on this journey of life.

The things that have happened to protect me or support me can be put in a separate chapter. People are not aware of their presence and what it has meant to me by them just being there at the time of need.

After I reported the incident, people I knew are coming into my path. No one knew what happened to me. Having been silent for so long and now bringing it to the light, I am interested in how people saw me back then. I need more information, more memories to go any further, but it is certainly taken seriously. The police said it was a serious crime.

It was like I was being shown what to do. and fear would take over. I had experiences that got to the point it would have been easier to just do it. Death and resurrection experiences included events such as the sexual abuse, divorce, and the death of my husband. I found that there is hope for the future and as I trusted God there was healing of the past events.

If I was adhering to the social norm of my peers, I would be in what is called God's waiting room. I do not consider my age indicates what I can do. I have found out that age is only a number. After retirement I not only went back to work but also continued studying.

Looking back over my life, I believe that my ability to make a difference was instilled in me as a young child. My mother was one of four children, (an older half-brother and two sisters); my father was one of ten children. My father came from a farming background and my mother came from a fishing background. My parents were married in 1941. Their living arrangements were with extended families before moving to their own home in the year, 1950. Their family was complete with seven children.

Our family helped many a battler. When another person came home for a meal dad would say to my mother, "Have you found another stray" There was always enough food to give another person a meal. Life is full of challenges and I do believe there is a new door opening for us to walk through after a period of pain.

I believe God has been drawn me to where I have been meant to be. I have been shown an area to work on from the past. The spirit was telling me to report the abuse, but I kept thinking it wasn't that bad. Other people have worse things that happen to them than I did. It so long ago and in the "too hard" basket but I was being reminded often when the person's name was mentioned in many conversations. If I was travelling, and mentioned where I grew up invariably I was asked if I knew him. I telephoned to talk to a crisis line and I was told I was to report it if I knew he was near anyone under eighteen. I went to visit a family and this lady had his nieces and nephew there. To top it off, he came into a doctor's waiting room and sat two seats from me. After I reported it his name had only been mentioned once.

There were many seasons in my life and sometimes I didn't know why. However, I found once one season is over and has been dealt with it, frees up a new thing to take place. One season has to be dealt with before the next one.

I had resigned from a job I had been working as a casual. I was looking for a new direction when I found myself walking through a shopping centre wondering what I was going to do. It was definitely one of those Holy Spirit moments and an answer to prayer. A young lady spoke to me about a college nearby who were taking new students. After getting information and a telephone number I telephoned and was given an appointment. After I was accepted I spoke to two friends who were also around seventy years old. From there the three of us went back to further education. It was that I was open to something new. Age has no barrier to a new beginning.

Why I wrote this book

I have wanted to leave a legacy to my children and hope that they will gain insights on their mother as a person. I have wanted to make a difference in what I have achieved. There has been some turbulence, but I have been being resilient on the way to the destination. I've kept focused on my spirit with peace, hope, and love. While moving from one season to the other, I have come to realise not to accumulate things. I could not take too much baggage with me. Taking stock of where I was at by reflecting and moving on, taking only what was needed for the next stage in life. With every challenge, there have been lessons to learn. The lessons can be gifts, and I come to know how to appreciate the gifts that I have been given.

I was open to opportunities. I found a card with the words that was just what I needed at the time.

"When one door of happiness closes; another opens; But often we look so long at the closed door that we do not see the one that has been open for us."
-Helen Keller.

Unexpectedly, I was invited to go with a group of young people to tour Turkey and Gallipoli. Visiting the war graves and being there, where it all happened, had an effect on me. I realised how young the boys were and began thinking of all the mothers and families in the hometowns. I saw lots of people and asked if they were tourists. I was told that they were off a cruise ship.

I had not thought about going on a cruise until I had a telephone call from a lady to ask if I wanted to go on a holiday with some other ladies. Without knowing or asking where we would be travelling to I said "Yes." We flew to Seattle, on the West Coast of the United States of America. We took a back to back cruise through Alaska and ending in Hawaii before flying back to Australia. I have since been on a number of cruises. If I have wanted to travel to a place and had no one to come with me I have found that cruising has been a safe way to travel while travelling on my own.

My father had been one of ten children, and I had a favourite aunty who was in her late nineties when I gathered enough information and had seventy pages of information printed and bound to take it to show my Aunty. I learnt while looking at family history during the First World War, about one of my great-Uncles had joined the armed forces and went to France. As a child, I would hear his name being mentioned. While growing up I thought he must have been alive when we lived as an extended family in my early years. However, it was while doing family history I came across information about his death in France. I had made arrangements to visit her the following week. However during that week my Aunty passed away. I have since been to France and was able to find his headstone; and spend time at the cemetery. I told the guide that I had the information printed and planned to go to France, but she died the following week, before I was able share the completed project with her.

The guide said an interesting thing. He has seen it many times: the family mantle being put on someone to visit the gravesite. It is like the person is being acknowledged, and there can be peace.

In recent years, I have learnt to play Canasta a card game called hand and foot. When I was growing up, all the family would play card games and board games. I was a girl, and there were things a girl didn't do. I would be sent to my room to read while I listened to the rest of the family having fun in the next room. I have finally been taught how to play euchre. I enjoy being on a team for tenpin bowling; it's been lots of fun and laughter.

As a child, I thought no one would believe me if I were to tell anyone what happened. As an adult, those very words that were spoken to me "We didn't believe you." It is no wonder we are being told just what we think someone wants to hear. Sometimes we don't hear about the journeys until it is too late. Then we start asking ourselves why?

Faith can move mountains. Intuition tells me when there is something that is not right. Learning to trust my instincts and allow it to guide me. As I hold on to my faith and moving forward knowing that the Lord has gone before me and is directing my path. I have come to know how to be responsible for my life and to allow others to be responsible for their lives. Focus on the good things by focusing on the good in situations. I celebrate life and am happy. Friendship has been important. However, some whom I thought were friends have told me that "We Didn't Believe You."

At home, I have been reconnecting with friends and spending time with family. As I recall memories of the past, I have written it down to complete this book. I am learning to leave the past behind and look for what the future holds. I keep the faith and stay true to self, loving life and seek the will of God in all that I do.

About the author

Joan Green was born mid 1940s in a small country town in New South Wales, Australia. Joan was one of seven children; the third child of a family of five brothers and one younger sister. Joan remembers the happy times including the special preparations that were made for Christmas and birthday teas.

Joan has a strong faith and a love for God. As a child wanted to be a teacher and do missionary work within the community. She was passionately drawn to the ministry of pastoral care. Due to circumstances life took a different journey.

Joan left school at sixteen and was a student nurse for three years before working as a cook, housemaid, waitressing, service station attendant, and process worker in a factory. When Joan turned twenty one she went to work on the railways. Joan realised no matter wherever she was working she was content.

Joan married at twenty two and had two daughters during that marriage which ended in divorce after sixteen years. After the birth of her second child the family moved back to the city. Joan made a decision due to the circumstance not to work but to spend time bringing up her two daughters. Although there were many challenges Joan enjoyed being a homemaker.

Joan married a second time to a fellow Christian, which sadly ended in divorce two years later. It was while Joan was studying that her third husband died by suicide just before their tenth wedding anniversary. Joan completed her studies and wrote a thesis.

Fifty-four years after a traumatic event at the age of nine, Joan reported it to the police. This book has come out of her journey to get to the stage where she could not only talk about it but had a voice that was heard.

Joan enjoys travelling, bushwalking, reading and theatre. One of the highlights of her travels has been to England and found the small village where her paternal grandfather was born and France to visit the battlefield where a Great Uncle is buried. One of the highlights of her travels was visiting a small village in England where her paternal grandfather was born. Another very memorable journey was visiting the battlefields in France where a Great Uncle was laid to rest, after losing his life in battle during the first-world war.

CPSIA information can be obtained
at www.ICGtesting.com
Printed in the USA
BVHW041801030820
585324BV00014B/859

9 781951 795009